21st Century Surrealism
A Guide for Artists and Creative People

21st Century Surrealism
A Guide for Artists and Creative People

by
Mark Sheeky

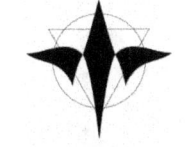

Pentangel Books

21st Century Surrealism
A Guide for Artists and Creative People

Written by Mark Sheeky.

With many thanks to Deborah Edgeley for proofreading, technical assistance in the realm of writing, and for endless support.

Illustrations and graphic design by Mark Sheeky.

1st edition, published in by Pentangel Books.
www.pentangel.co.uk
ISBN 978-0-9571947-6-2

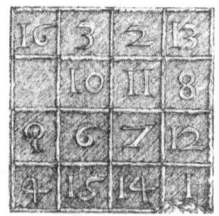

To the riff-raff who make a profession of thinking,
and to all of you with open ears - please feel it.

CONTENTS

THE MYSTERIOUS ISLAND

A STUDY OF SCARLET

THE TOMB

THE GARDENS OF ELYSIUM

THE BOUNDLESS OCEAN

NOTES

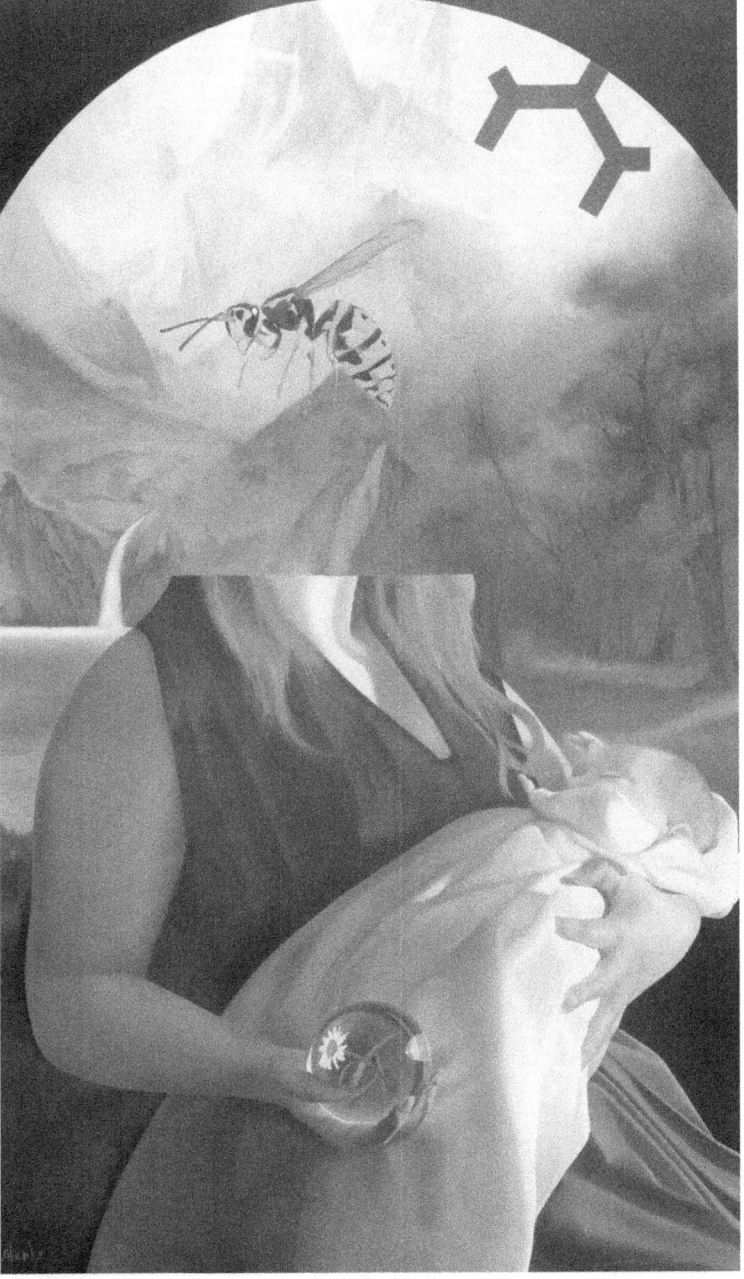

THE MYSTERIOUS ISLAND

21st CENTURY SURREALISM

THE MYSTERIOUS ISLAND

Surrealism

Old surrealism[1], vast and powerful like the ocean fire of the soul, flowing crystal of creativity that spans the 20th century like ten ten-fingered skeletal hands. Let us grasp the thin, sallow hand of the Comte de Lautrémont and pull the peat threads of this floor apart. Let us detangle the tobacco scents of history and peer at the curious concepts of some communist dreamers, the surrealists. It is the dawn of the 21st century, one hundred years since the Surrealist Revolution, and art is presently ubiquitous and lost; vomiting emotionless turgid decoration of the New Puritan order over the new stainless-steel-religious marvel of the global computer network. Its witch-fire intolerance for the extraordinary is itself extraordinary. The world is revolutionary and art is not.

Sigmund Freud, artist, and André Breton, poet, curator, socialist conquistador, pioneered an expedition into the verdant jungles of the human mind, determined to discover and share a new El Dorado that might liberate humanity from the yoke of its daily fears and mediocrity, yet the city was a myth and the gold as transparent and elusive as saline breath. Now, today, the wet forests of the mind are still unmapped, yet psychology quickly moved on and made great advancements in the 20th century. Surrealism; the first true art experiment, unique as an art form in its rigour for scientific analysis, in publication of results, in exploring the role of creativity as a tool for social transformation, did not move on, remaining trapped in a box, or perhaps a curious drawer, in the nineteen-thirties. Why? Why didn't the art of the mind continue to advance in tangent with the advances of its psychological sibling? There were many reasons, not least political; minuscule global squabbles, group tiffs, and perhaps a simple conclusion that everything had been done - truly the most horrific four words in art, those uttered only through thick oil by the most vomitating of octopuses. No, no!

Surrealist concepts now permeate through all of art, but they always had. Breton's strength was as curator, writer, and analyst of good taste, and his analysis of historical art trends and his contemporaneous mental Zeitgeist, helped define fantastical ideas in emotional terms; separating the whim from the visceral. The explorations of mind became self-centred and defined as indeterminate, unfathomable, expressionistic. To question them was like questioning Schroedinger's Cat about its health.

Today, the human mind still exists: the unconscious (whatever that is), the conscious (whatever that is), feelings (whatever they are), representations of reality (whatever that is), and the relationships between these things. These powerful tools for artistic expression need sharpening. Visual art has achieved its totality in the way that music had by the middle of the 20th century. Music began as an abstract form centuries earlier; all music became surrealistic to some extent; the zinc tubes of Bach programmed with divine quantum proportions. The time is right to analyse the mind and the silvery cabinets of creativity, lined with their plush velvet delights.

Come! I see that your matted black hair is being ripped by the wet wind, the grey hail of this wintery dawn.

Come, Maldoror, with your dark eyes, your twisted yellow nails. Let us grasp *The Wings of Love* and tear them apart with our pointed teeth while Beverly Moss[2] protests.

The jungle awaits.

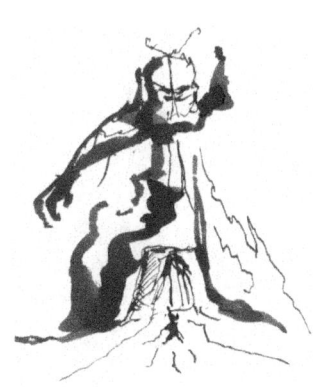

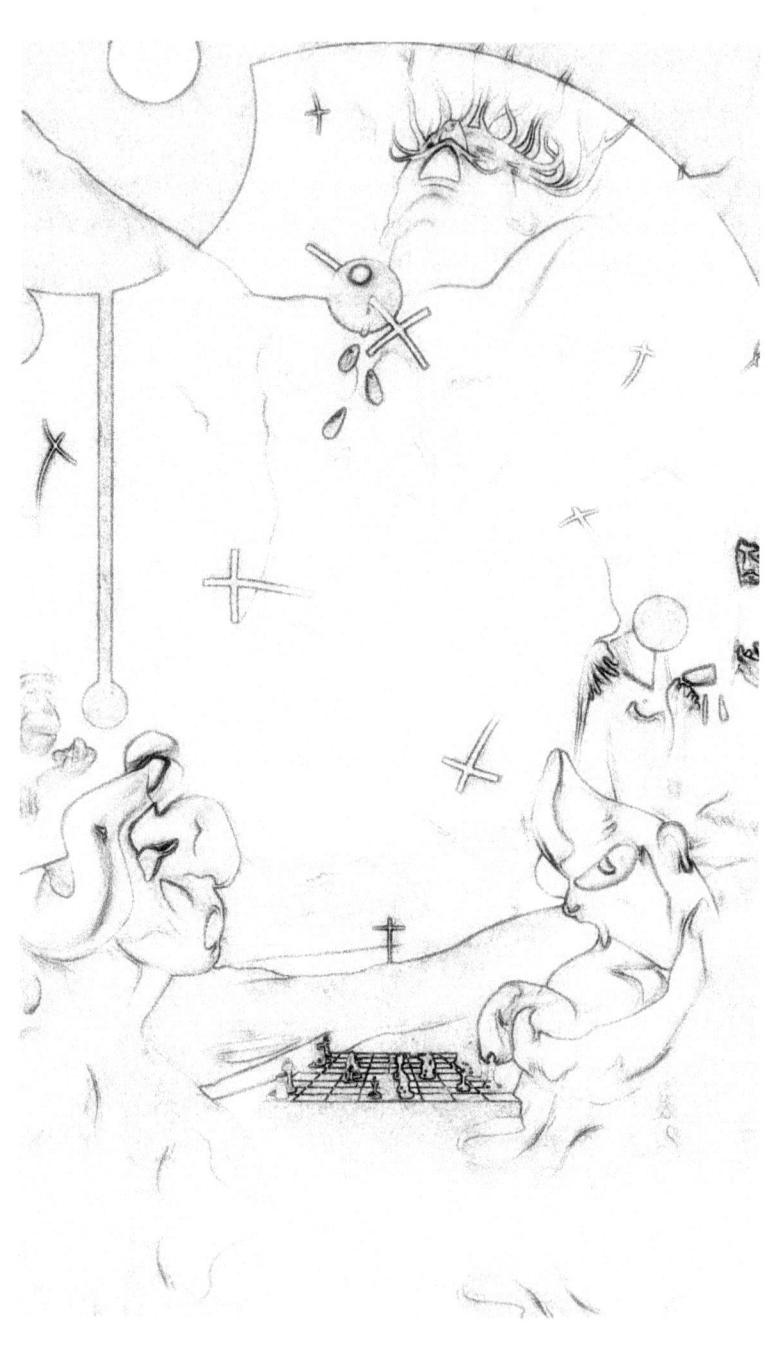

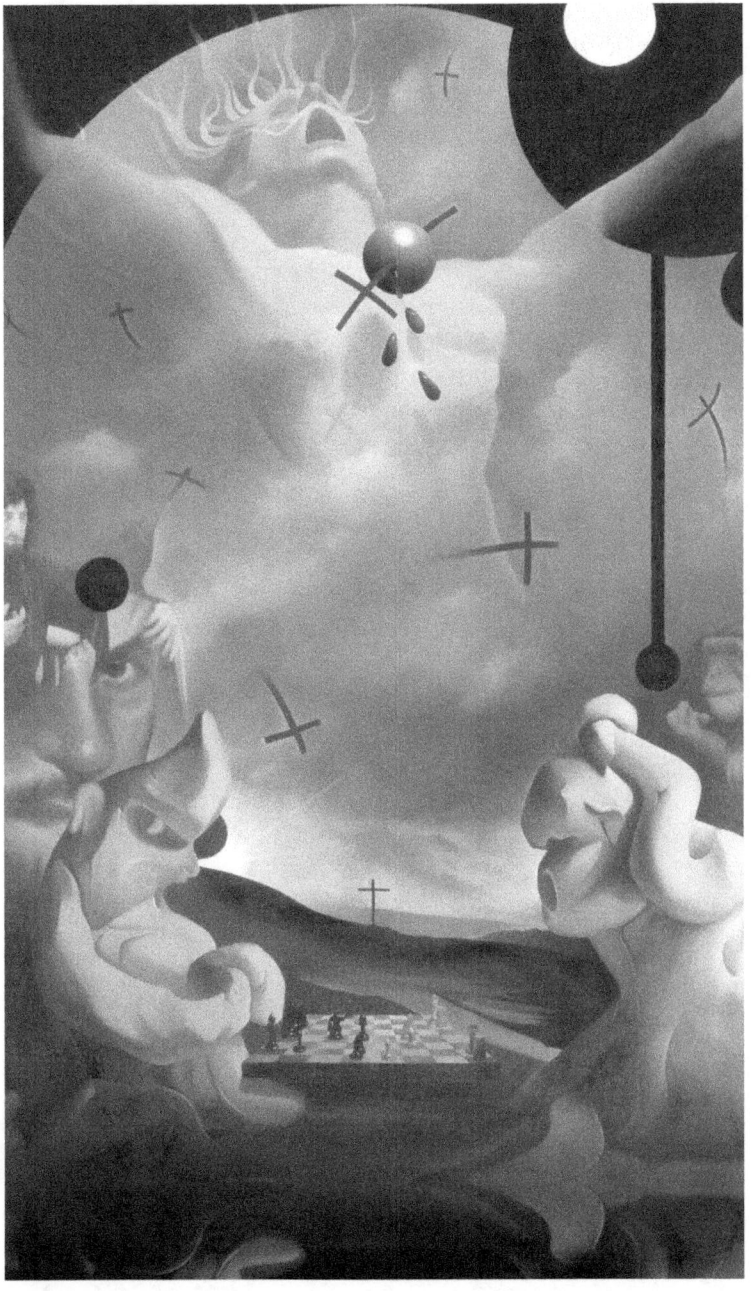

A STUDY OF SCARLET

21st CENTURY SURREALISM

A STUDY OF SCARLET

History

Existence is elsewhere. The perfect start, for these three words ended the first surrealist manifesto and welcome our entry into this quaint Victorian study, a room of warm wood and the textures of wax history.

The artist, like any visionary, should always look towards the future, which is always better than the past. Nostalgia is a form of self-comfort. Comfort is rest, peace, decay. To create is to be active, energetic, brave, forward looking. Always moving forwards. It's debatable whether we have more control over the past or the future. We can re-imagine the past and change our memories, and we can rewrite history, yet our future is set onto an inevitable path, don't you think?

Nostalgia is decay. Yet, it is only by picking apart the fibres of the past that we can mould them into the beautiful things of the future. Life is about replication and correction. All things do this, atoms; deoxyribonucleic acid, society.

So, let us step back, back through the halls, down the dark corridors, the browned echoes of soil. Back through the yellowed photographs, the prickly sack-cloths and clove scents of the era before the Second World War, the lull of waking between the two sleeps of each war.

"Man, that inveterate dreamer, daily more discontent with his destiny, has trouble assessing the objects he has been led to use, objects that his nonchalance has brought his way."[1]

The *Manifesto of Surrealism* was a call for internal examination, a plan set out to release the forces of imagination in a conservative world. Its driving force was the conquest of repression, a revolution against tedium, conformity, normality, in world seething with subdued emotions. Society, then, acted automatically, robotically and consciously, rather than upon its strange emotions, which were perhaps scarred by the Great War, and, as such, uncertain. Society will always have repressive elements, and always be constraining to the imagination because society is an average, a mean, a median, and the exceptional will necessarily be different; exceptional people and exceptional ideas.

The hope of the original surrealists was for a new path of social change, revolution through the unleashing of personal imaginative power. This could be achieved purely by the application of psychology, for it was thought that each person contained an informational core that could be tapped and programmed to transform us, and society, into a world of happiness, contentment and peace. Such were the dreams of communists.

The tweed-constructed philosopher, that inveterate dreamer embodied, Sigmund Freud, created a theory of dreams that codified the concept of a common psychological language. For the surrealists, the first stage of the liberation of mankind was to explore it, releasing the unconscious, a secret world of desires and repressed fantasies. The unconscious was, and is, truly imaginative, capable of infinite desires; and the most powerful of these desires were expressed as reprehensible acts, unacceptable sexual acts, and anything else which could not be expressed in normal daily lives. This was the essential component, for to express these feelings and desires would destroy them, and like vampires in the sunlight they would fade away. A repressive social regime feeds the unconscious of society, and the more repressed a regime, and the more limited an individual in ability to express, the more powerful the unconscious becomes, the louder it screams.

The imaginative powers of the repressed mind were recognised and identified in the great art of the past. This was compared to the turgid and dead art of the contemporaneous present, for an essential component of the art of the unconscious was that it was not expressed because it was not socially acceptable. Like a pickle or spirit, the ideas would ferment. This meant that the best art, the most revolutionary art, was in a minority and would not gain mass popularity; or at least, it could not be conservative and polite. The art of the unconscious must essentially be constructed from socially unacceptable ideas.

Now here is a universal truth; even in revolutionary times there are ideas and behaviours that are not acceptable. The development of what is and what is not acceptable is learned by us over our lifetimes, and particularly during our childhood. Of course, what is socially acceptable changes all of the time, so we suppress that which is not. It is the suppression of these ideas that causes them to grow, calling for our attention with increasingly loud voices. Our ancient and deep minds cry out behavioural messages from our youthful, and so distant, cells, sending them swimming up through thick seaweeds of brain, weeds that act like curious lenses, distorting each message in creative and unexpected ways in order to grab our attention. These ideas will always have emotional impact; they were repressed because they are a jarring alternative to social normality, and their root will be a personal truth, an ignored or misunderstood message of how we should be behaving.

The cry of the repressed unconscious is essentially a spark of absolute honesty, of true personal reality, and it is necessarily startling and different. It is something emotional, because it will clash with the feelings of our society. It is something imaginative because the mind will fight to draw attention to itself as loudly as it can. Good art is art that is emotional, and imaginative, and authentic, and this is why surrealism was and remains and will always remain the most powerful creative concept in art.

It is only now, with our great eyes of knowledge cast over history, that this fundamental point can be understood. In actual history, things were not always so clear. The ideas and understandings of the workings of the human mind were shrouded in mystery as little as a century ago. To many people, this is still a mystery. Where did things go wrong?

We might start by considering that Sigmund Freud's interpretation of dreams postulated that certain images and symbols in dreams represented different things, different ideas, and that these objects created a common symbolic language. The concept led to the creation of 'dream dictionaries', which persist as curiosities to this day. Naturally, this language stemmed from repressed desires, and so concerned everything that was deemed unacceptable by the society of those days. It was reasonable to assume that the repressions of the day would always represent problems for humanity, and that therefore a common series of mental problems could be diagnosed and addressed based on these feelings and symbols.

A common symbolic language is obviously a flawed idea. Times change, and so do the things which are considered socially unacceptable, so the meaning of different symbols and feelings will vary over time. Also, each of us accumulates a different symbolic language based on our personal experiences; a telephone might mean one thing to one person, and another thing to another, or not even exist in their world. This, combined with the social context of the day, makes the interpretation of an unconscious image or dream difficult, or perhaps even impossible. One great irony of dreams is that only the dreamer can really understand their meaning, and yet, even this doesn't always happen.

Both of these factors combine to disrupt the concept of a universal mental language; but it is never totally destroyed. Knowing about the dreamer and his or her society can allow us to construct an interpretation of an unconscious image, even when baffling, and many symbols are common and within the range of experience for even the majority of humanity; the sea, the sky, the sun, the moon, love, sadness, and a panoply of animals.

For an artist, however, bafflement is never a good emotion to portray. In feeling and meaning, it should be clear what an artwork means and why, and that feeling and meaning should be stated powerfully. Confusion and anxious chaos tells us nothing because it contains no useful information. It is the same, but at the opposite extreme, as emotionlessness.

The meaning of a symbol changes over time. Shakespeare's gilded lilies may one day be extinct, like the exact meaning of Malvolio's stockings. Leonardo da Vinci's yarn-winder[2] might one day be little more than a stick.

Oh, the parade of the nonsensical object! Confusion and emotionless death: the Scylla and Charybdis of art! In a world of creative power, from robot brains, to kittens hooked to electroencephalographs, how are we to tell what is genuinely an unconscious, imaginative symbol of great art, an explosion of original, truthful, authentic human expression? How can we discern a cry of anguish and torment from any old space-angel?

Authenticity and truth are often considered the mark of good art; why? Could not a pretty, even cute scene, be good art? Perhaps one with a vast panoply of imagination, technical skill and fantasy on display?

No. The reason is simple: that a repressed cry is essentially rebellious, essentially disruptive, and essentially unacceptable to social normality. Art that is harmonious to society is bad art. Art which is nice is bad art. Good art is uncomfortable.

But wait, this is a bold statement. What art is, and what good art should be, is a vast topic. Also, there are many examples of great art which is not uncomfortable or rebellious or disruptive, from Shakespeare's *The Tempest* to Beethoven's Fifth Symphony.

Again, no, answers our dialectical echo. Those works, like any great work, were uncomfortable, rebellious, disruptive in their time, and it is through their greatness that they remain so now. The content of those works, and any great creative work, is that it is continually rebellious and passionate, setting and disrupting moods, creating its own society and fighting inside it. This factor is the genius present in all timeless masterpieces.

But, great art needn't always be timeless. Often the most powerful emotions and most powerful artworks are those that rebel against the prevailing mood of society. It is through that strong contrast that they gain their power. Can a 'cute' image, a 'nice' thing, a calm and pretty thing ever be good art, then? Of course: in a society where such things are not permitted. In an ugly world, beauty is revolutionary. In a beautiful world, ugliness is revolutionary. In times of war, peace is revolutionary. In times of peace, war is revolutionary.

But now, let us relax, relax. Let the smoke of history spiral in blue waltzes, up to an infinite star. Let our liquid limbs hang loose and pour from our tired shoulders, towards the warm floor. The vast topic about what art is, and what good art should be is not so vast. It can be defined and refined clearly and efficiently in a mere twenty-five thousand words, or less.

Now we must relax, for it is time to crack the sky with light-ning. The aim of this opening text was to resurrect the vital spark of surrealism and its greatest contribution to art, that of releasing imagination, and, when doing so, psychologically helping the artist, and the psychological well-being of society. Perhaps this Golem is not so dead, after all.

Zeus casts his bolt.

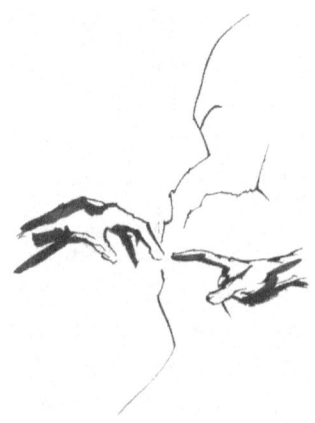

Creativity

"I have always been amazed at the way an ordinary observer lends so much more credence and attaches so much more importance to waking events than to those occurring in dreams."[1]

Thus spake André Breton (or rather wrake, wroke, wrote). The very word 'dream' means to imagine, to muse. We can dream of a great future, and often do; people rarely 'have a dream' that is doomed somehow. To dream is to aspire, and so dreams, the word in English at least, is fundamentally linked with a positive force for creativity and imagination.

The lightning of Zeus strikes a marble altar. Upon it were carved the letters 'SIGMUND FREUD'. It explodes into a thousand fist-sized chunks.

Creative imaginative thought, is after all, the goal of an artist, is it not? Is it possible to be an artist, a good one, and not be creative?

No. The very role of artist is that of creator; that is its definition. The more creative an artist is, the better he or she is as an artist. The supreme artist is infinitely creative. Artists, in the tedium of actual life, are often specialists, but this is only due to a limited capacity for work and mastery of a certain skill. The ideal artist is a generalist; a master of all skills and all media, and infinitely creative.

The creative idea is any thought that differs from consensus. The more creative the idea, the more it differs from the consensus view. This reinforces the broad thrust of our earlier revelations on art; that good art is rebellious.

This understanding has important implications for artists because art is an industry driven by creativity, and industry, as a faculty of capitalism, which, when ideal, is the practical, logical expression of the natural psychology of humankind, depends partly on popularity.

At its most extreme, an artist must choose between a creative idea, which is unpopular, or a popular idea that is uncreative. Working artists tend to need a degree of popularity to survive. There are many more uncreative artists successfully creating their mediocre, mainstream, poor artworks, than genuinely creative artists. The genuinely creative artists are necessarily working on unpopular ideas. Of course, not all unpopular ideas are good art, but they are always creative, and so, on some level, we could say that they are created by good artists. This at least indicates that a great artist can create terrible art. Great artists beware.

One must ask, what benefit does the supremely creative idea have if it is unpopular with everyone? Well, not all creative ideas are good art. There are many factors in a good work of art, creativity is but one, but one can say that an uncreative idea creates bad art. Using this logic, you can recognise bad art by its very popularity; bad art is popular as soon as it is born.

But of course, this can't always be the case because some good art is popular, and masterpieces can remain popular, as well as excellent works of art, for centuries. There are several reasons why this is the case:

Firstly, these great works were creative once. These began as obscure and original, and grew to become popular. These pioneer works are often imitated, and sometimes surpassed by their imitators, but the first new work in a series or genus always holds a special power because of its seed of originality.

Secondly, like the emotional contrast present within a great artwork, it can also contain new creativity within it; be of sufficient size, complexity, and originality, that new depth, new ideas, and new revolutions can be discovered and uncovered within it again and again. This is another factor of genius present in all timeless masterpieces.

It is also an important function of art that it drives trends. Art creates new, unpopular ideas, which become popular. Things that begin as popular, that fit in, that are normal, can never create a trend or instigate change. This is why creativity is important for society, it is the embryo of the future. Change is inevitable, and the creative idea determines what things change into.

I gaze up to the red grey storm clouds, dark and foaming. They boil like a vast brain.

When do we, as humans, as apes, need to be creative?

When we need to decide whether to fight or flee. When we need to find food or shelter or some other thing for our survival. When we need to make a choice. We need creativity when automatic thought is not an option. Conscious thought exists so that we can be creative.

In one sentence I have proved that the purpose of thought itself is art.

It is a curious fact that we appear to be more creative when hungry; Breton mentioned this briefly in his surrealist manifesto[3], and a hormone produced when we are hungry, ghrelin, appears to stimulate learning and memory. Starvation is a life or death situation that demands adept thinking, so this makes sense.

Look! A gap in the clouds.

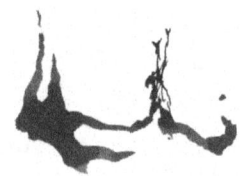

Consciousness

Consciousness, that most simple and obvious property of being which we all possess, like love and fear, seems to be a mysterious phantom, uncertain, and difficult to explain. We can never be certain that other people are conscious, or other animals, or other things. If a computer writes "I think, therefore I am" upon its screen, then we would probably not accept that it is indeed thinking.

There are several aspects to conscious thought. What we call being conscious could mean being awake or aware, or experiencing the world, or thinking. We could say that being asleep and dreaming fits many of the descriptions of consciousness; if we were born and lived our entire lives in a dream world, would we think of ourselves as conscious? Perhaps. Perhaps not.

So what is consciousness? There are a four main aspects which we can touch upon: our senses of the external world, our senses of our internal thoughts, the ability to choose to focus on one or more thoughts over others, and the unique perspective that is being.

The unique perspective that is being is a strange one. It seems that we have a unique view of the universe. We can never know what it would be like to be another person, or to be a butterfly, for example, but perhaps our view is only there because of what we know and where we are. If we sliced our bodies apart at the waist (eww) but remained alive, then we would, I presume, assume that our top half was our conscious half. If we sliced our bodies vertically, leaving an eye in each half, then which would we be? I suppose we could be two people then, each with some fragments of our former self, but surely our legs in the first example would feel that too, and yet feel aggrieved that their half lacked eyes! Humans are very sight orientated creatures, which itself taints that thought experiment. A unique perspective of being is surely only a part of being in any one place with limited information. The television in the corner has a unique perspective. It has a memory because it can remember the last channel. It has senses because it has switches that can detect being pressed. It's a unique being. It can never know what we feel like and we can never know what it feels like. So it seems that a unique perspective isn't part of consciousness, but part of existence, and applies to everything.

Still, we, as people, have a natural idea of what consciousness is, what active intelligent thought is. We can use our senses, our sight, hearing etc. to detect that others too are thinking, and so it is through those media that we discern conscious intelligence in others.

When we are asleep, but not dreaming, we are not conscious. For us this is the same as death. It should now be noted that if life between dreams does not exist, then the existence of life after death is exceptionally precarious. It should also be noted, by counter-argument, that while people are remembered and while the impact of their actions are felt, they can still be influential, and therefore still live, to those extents, beyond death.

Conscious thought consists of our awareness of our current state via our senses, and an awareness of our memories and mental processes. Descartes may have considered his senses unreliable, but there is no evidence that our senses of our own thoughts or recollections are more reliable than our eyes, ears, etc. In terms of what thinking is, the sense of thinking is all that matters, rather than its accuracy (perhaps in this case we are thinking about thinking, thus making this statement para-doxical, however, I don't want to spiral into philosophical infinities; if you don't believe that you are thinking or con-scious, then note that by considering that question you have proved yourself wrong, and so can continue reading with con-fidence).

What senses of our thoughts do we have? We can close our eyes and see pictures in our minds, so we have a mental eye. We can hear music in our heads, so we have a mental ear. So, we have external and internal senses. Do we have the same of each?

Here's a better question: can we have any thoughts that don't reference any of our senses? Well, we can have loves and pains and beliefs, and things like that, but they are still sensual things. All we need to know is that those things, like any thought, can be communicated, pondered and expressed. That is what defines what a thought is; its ability to be communic-ated. We might not be able to point to a body part and say that it is the anguish detection organ, yet we can transmit anguish with ordinary senses, and pick up anguish or other complex feelings from others, with ordinary senses.

To help illustrate this more clearly, let us temporarily become a chess computer.

A chess computer has the sense of the board, and the position of the pieces. All of its thoughts concern it. It has a program too, a flow of information, like water flowing in pipes controlled with valves, for that is all that a computer program is. The pipes could wind and wend and bend all over the place, but it can only perceive in chess positions, and only express itself in chess moves. If it can only talk to the world in this way, it can only talk to itself in this way; remember, the chess position detector is its only sense. It isn't capable of perceiving any thought that is not a chess position. Perhaps, one day, it could discern aspects of its program by analysing how it moves when playing a chess game, but if it did, it could only tell itself, or the world, its conclusions using the medium of chess positions.

Our dear chess computer has been programmed to be vigilant about threats to its queen, its most treasured piece, so positions that threaten her cause it anxiety. It could express this anxiety by showing us a chess position that threatens the queen. We humans wouldn't pick up its feeling, but another chess computer like it would see this position, recognise it, and detect the anxiety. It is in this way that the pure exchange of sensory information can transmit anxiety, love, confidence, flirtatiousness, jealousy, belief, or any complex feeling, with just basic senses. A good book can transmit those things, plain written words, so clearly a full gamut of senses are not needed to transmit complex emotions. Some of these feelings may be more inherent to being human, some might be cultural; but among peers, that information can be exchanged. When we communicate those things to people who are not like us, such as our friend the chess computer transmitting to us its joy of a certain impending check-mate, they might never understand.

So, to take our examinations to their ultimate, logical conclusion, our thoughts are conversations with different parts of us, and they are made in images, sounds, feelings, and every normal, everyday sense that we would recognise, and only that. Our internal senses do reflect all of our external ones; we have a mind's eye, a mind's ear, a mind's feel, and everything else.

When thinking, we are only aware of a tiny fragment of thought at once; one thing, like a word on a page in a sentence. We have a memory of the sentence so far, and so can discern something about the information flow of our minds, and we might be preparing on some level for the up-and-coming words. In another part of our heads we have a sense of free thought, a feeling that we can dart to a new sentence if desired.

It's a curious fact that we can make choices at every moment, yet only certain moments are thought of as choices. It is as though the river of our thoughts flows naturally onwards, and that we have to get up and use energy to divert it, and so we pay attention to our river only when we can see that it needs diverting left or right.

In a busy day we have several mental books to hand, several

books of thoughts within reach, at our mental fingertips. We can grab these books at will, and turn our thinking towards them.

Beyond those books are other books, slightly at further reach, forming part of the vast library of our mind that contains all of our knowledge as a human being. We are born with some books intact and written, an innate knowledge or instinct, written in the womb. Most of the books are, apparently, ours; written and filed as we live, learn, and experience things.

These books might not all be in our brains, but can be stored in our muscles, our nerves, our cells too; but also in our actual diaries, in our friends, our workplaces, and in global computer networks. The knowledge we have at our fingertips can span from tiny, instinctive fragments of thought, such as the know-ledge to micro-move the pupils of our darting eye sockets, through to the vast panoply of the Internet.

Conscious awareness is merely the act of accessing some of that knowledge and being aware of it.

The feeling of freedom to direct our minds to any thought we choose is part of being conscious, too: we can think of ele-phants, if we choose, of the Arctic ocean, if we choose. Also, by extension, we can access knowledge with our bodies too: by reading our diaries, if we choose, by asking our friends, if we choose. By this extension we have expanded our con-sciousness out of our bodies and into the real world. Because of this, in terms of thought and action, there are no borders between what is physical, and that which is mental.

At this point, 'dualist' philosophers, who believe in a separation between mind and body, may explode into a million bits of awe at my perfect solution to the so-called Mind-Body Problem (of course, they will be aware of many philosophers' similar claims, which I must assume are not as elegant as mine). I will ignore this because it wasn't my intention to philosophise; my aim was to take a quick look at what we consider conscious and unconscious thought, and how these relate to creativity. Philosophers who don't accept that free will exists (I may well agree with them) can pretend that creative thought is possible. If everything is pre-destined (I would probably agree with this too) then such a pretence will make no difference.

Ah, creativity. The ability to choose what we think is creativity. We can choose it from any of our books; that is the scope of our creativity. Laziness is choosing a nearby book. It takes more work to find a distant book that we haven't used in a while.

The Unconscious

Most of the writing, filing, and sorting of the books in our minds happens beyond our conscious awareness, as though an invisible librarian is constantly ordering the vast catalogue of our knowledge. If you consider that you can read one word of one sentence each day; this fleeting thing we call conscious thinking, and then consider all of what you actually know, then it becomes obvious that the great majority of the ordering process; to write, to file, and store that vast library of our knowledge, must happen in the shadowed background of our minds.

This filing process takes place constantly; well, perhaps it does, it is beyond our awareness, so by definition we cannot ever tell. At the very least, every memory must be recorded, that's what memory means. Every recollection of a memory is recorded too; we don't remember what we don't recall. Do unrecalled memories exist? Yes, but only if and when we recall them. We can't say that they certainly exist when we don't recall them; in that circumstance they are identical to not being there at all. This principle of bringing into existence by observation seems to reflect a quantum-mechanical principle that something exists to the extent it is perceived.

It is clear that our experience of being conscious involves a sense of our own thoughts and memories, not just the sensory experiences of the outside world.

Consider every sense you have; sight, smell, hearing, touch, taste, and how active each sense is at each minute of the day, and how many memories of each sense must be created. It is only then that you can consider the enormity of the work that the human brain must complete, and all without your tiny fragment of experience of the now that we call consciousness.

The word 'unconscious' has been used over and over again, and even in today's English it can refer to people who look asleep, or are sedated, as well as thoughts that we are not aware of. Here, I define it as those thoughts, those automatic and indirectable actions of the invisible librarian.

If unconscious thoughts are indirectable and not subject to our control, are they creative? Isn't creativity the ability to assess and choose something consciously?

There are degrees of awareness and freedom to control. Is control necessary for creativity? Perhaps one of the main benefits of unconscious creation is that is it not directly controlled, although we can't tell if unconscious thoughts are controlled or not, because, well, they are unconscious, and beyond the gaze of our mental senses. Can we have free will without awareness of it?

No. Free will is the sensation and feeling of being in control, and little else. The river of our thoughts flows. If we are unable to see the river and have no awareness of any control over its direction, then the point seems moot. The path of our unconscious thoughts surely flows in some direction, but if we are not aware of that direction, then any secret ways in which we

are changing its path are, perhaps, unimportant; but only perhaps. We might have some influence over an unseen process,
but merely be unable to predict or determine any outcome.
This might be like a blind man prodding the driver of a coach
and horses. He might be able to influence the journey, but
know little else about it.

Perhaps though, there are other clues that we don't have control over our unconscious minds, clues that emerge in the
world of dreams.

Control or intelligence aren't always useful for creativity, and
perhaps the element of chance, or the very lack of willpower, is
what is beneficial to the artist. A machine can be creative in
this way, even an object with no intelligence at all. Drop a
glass cup; its fragments form a pattern. Some curatorial control
is necessary to filter what is a meaningful pattern, and what is
not, but the cup itself constituted an important new source of
information.

Apart from its capacity for a spontaneity untrammelled by will,
the unconscious can be more inventive than our conscious
minds because it has access to a vast panoply of source information, far larger than the surface pages that our daily minds
flick though. There are levels to our thoughts, with immediate
thoughts and memories occupying our immediate times, those
things which skim lightly over the hot surface of our boiling
star minds. Then there are slightly more distant thoughts that
take slightly longer to reach, then more distant thoughts and
memories, and more, deeper and deeper. The deep thoughts

are too far away for us to think with fast enough to be of daily use. Perhaps what we know as conscious awareness and control is simply a matter of access speed. If so, then those with more agile brains would literally be more conscious; they would have direct, fast access to more knowledge.

Can the conscious mind access anything that our unconscious can? Let us first remember that by conscious mind we can mean different things; our sense of thinking, our ability to choose what we think, etc.

Well, all of our mind can affect our lives, that is its purpose. If any part of it couldn't, it would be the same as that part not existing, so all parts our mind can certainly be brought, on some level, into our tangible experiences of the world.

But, can our mental gaze, our internal sense of thinking, access any part of our unconscious? If we are to attain full mastery of our imagination, then we need to be able to access it.

The answer is yes. There is no need to delve deeply to ascertain this; the facts are simple and obvious. Everything we think is a memory, even our physical actions. A nearby pen is fast to grab, as adults our motor skills have learned this. A more advanced skill like playing a guitar might take more time. These things have exact mental analogues. A recent or well practised memory is fast to recall. A more distant or more clumsy memory is more difficult, like a new skill being learned, it takes more physical time to actually remember the less-well-trodden memories. The distant volumes of our brains drift in and out of reach of our mental fingertips.

We can be aware of our thoughts, and in control, to different degrees, and at many levels of speeds. If recalling a memory can take a long time, then storing memories in those distant archives must take a long time too.

But, dear traveller, I sense that you are growing weary. Let us rest, rest deeply in the soft arms of clouds. Let us float upon a river of mercury and golden moonbeams.

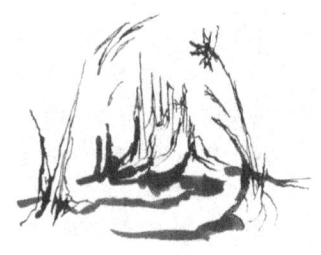

Dreams

"You do look, my son, in a moved sort, as if you were dis-may'd: be cheerful, sir. Our revels now are ended. These our actors, as I foretold you, were all spirits and are melted into air, into thin air: and, like the baseless fabric of this vision, the cloud-capp'd towers, the gorgeous palaces, the solemn temples, the great globe itself, ye all which it inherit, shall dissolve, and, like this insubstantial pageant faded. Leave not a rack behind. We are such stuff as dreams are made on, and our little life is rounded with a sleep."[4]

Conscious thought is both being aware of our thoughts and being in control of them. Can we be aware of thinking and have no control over what we think?

This happens to all of us in dreams, quite the most relaxing and worryless state. Dreams are, at their simplest, thoughts that happen without free will. We are generally not in conscious control of dreams directly, but lucid dreams can grant us full control of them, as though we were holographic gods. We can have degrees of lucidity too; dreams can often be guided by inkling feelings of what is going to happen next.

It's not necessary here, if it should ever be truly possible, to grasp at what or why dreams are. Like Prospero above, we dreamers know the answer. Neurologically, the latest science informs us that dreams are linked to memories and filing, as though our library, now dark because our external senses are dimmed, is seen by torchlight, casting a beam at the magically moving books of our knowledge that are being written and stored by the invisible librarian. Yet it is apparent, at least to this sorcerer, that dreaming can happen while awake too, and that messages from the more distant parts of our minds are being sent to us regularly.

Dreams have different degrees of strength and clarity. How can we know this? Firstly, if you will permit a subjective experience, sometimes I hardly remember my dreams, and reality is connected to memory. Things that are forever forgotten do not exist in our minds. Some dreams simply appear to be stronger than others, although we can train ourselves and tune our minds to recall and experience dreams more, or less, strongly.

Secondly, and perhaps more convincingly, sometimes dreams loudly impose themselves upon our waking minds in the form of hallucinations. These are thoughts without free will, exactly as dreams. Are there any aspects of hallucinations that are definably different from dreams, apart from the common acceptance that dreams occur when asleep?

No. If we were to report to a doctor that we hallucinated last night when asleep, this would be considered a dream in every respect. It is reasonable to suppose that dreams and hallucinations have the same mechanism of creation, and perhaps the same purpose.

Our waking dreams are not always loud, however. Some waking visions can be very pale, some more imposing. In the silent darkness of our crucible minds we can tune our mental ears and eyes to perceive these thoughts. For an artist, or indeed a mystic, this is a vital skill.

We each own a library, a vast array of knowledge built and stored over an entire lifetime. It is an amazingly powerful resource, and learning to tune in to our dreams, both sleeping and waking, is how we can access it.

Reader, we will do this later.

The Power of the Irrational

Among other things, surrealism was, and is, a rebellion against logic and rationality. It was, and is, a call to unleash the irrational and the bounded imagination. Why is the rational bad and the irrational good? One of the criticisms of surrealism is that it can produce nonsense, that it is actually designed to produce nonsense, or produce 'any old thing' that need not, can not, and should not, be explained.

Bah!

There is a crucial difference between 'any old thing' and a product of the unconscious; the latter has meaning, it is merely hidden. The former, a random object, has no meaning, like the bits of broken cup lying on the floor, like the shape of a handful of sand cast onto white paper. If we see things in these shapes, we add our meaning. The object and the patterns have no inherent meaning.

But, can the meaning that we, the audience, bring still result in art? Of course; and this cannot be avoided, but that art won't be as good, as rich in content, as it could be. Art is a form of communication between artist and audience. Emotional and intellectual information must be conveyed, and the artist should be directing what that information is. Art is a dialogue between two people; and just as polemics are bad art for being one-sided, a lack of substance is bad art for the same reason. Order must wrestle chaos in equal measure.

Why might an irrational idea be better than a rational, reasoned, one? Surely every creator, like an engineer, can use any product of mind, conscious and unconscious, to create?

This is true. Perhaps the answer depends on what is considered rational. The surrealist theory is that these thoughts, these which emerge via various 'automatic' or meditatory techniques, are the raw, unaltered outpourings of the mind and so contain more truth, whatever that is, than a processed or reasoned thought. Can we tell if this is actually the case?

No. There is no reason to assume that the unconscious mind is more or less honest than the conscious mind, and there is no way to check; but there is one important aspect of the irrational, or of any thought, that is not compromised by intellectual reasoning, that makes it better for art; it is more emotional, and art that is more emotional is better art.

An idea which is enigmatic, obscure, hidden, has more emotional power than an idea which is overt. Feelings, these simple and obvious things which even small children and animals can understand, cannot be completely explained in rational, logical terms. When we understand our feelings on a rational, emotionless level, they dissipate relative to that degree of understanding. Because of this, talking about our worries makes them go away, but even analysing them ourselves: with writing, art, or logic, will dissipate them. It is as though an emotion is a message to be acted on, sent in an abstracted form. Once the message is read, understood, acknowledged, it vanishes.

This means that the emotional power of a message depends partly on a lack of its comprehension, and creating that which is emotionally powerful depends on the presence of an enigmatic quality. It is for this reason that a concealed meaning is better than an overt one: it is more emotional. The irony of poetry is that rather than being a plain and direct form of communication, it subverts meaning with complicated language and awkwardness. This is why. It is through the enigmatic that the emotions in a poem can decay slowly like a fading cello.

A STUDY OF SCARLET

The Limits of Imagination

Imagination, wrapped in its increasingly comfortable strait-jacket. It must explode.

The release of the imagination was, and remains, a surrealist principle: to unleash, with revolutionary fervour, free thought in a conservative world. The real world is boring, tired, grey, and will always be conservative. Society will always have taboos. The mind is exciting, vivid, and filled with feelings and possibilities. Does this have taboos too?

It must, yes.

Is that really true, and are there limits to what we can imagine? This is an important question because any limits to our imagination has serious implications for artists, we who are driven by creativity, because as we've as good as proven: imaginative ideas are better than unimaginative ideas. To be as creative as possible, thought and imagination need to be as free as possible.

Well, we could start with the tour-de-force that was the earlier section about consciousness; I, ahem, we, practically proved that the philosophical bounds between thought in our heads, and action in the real world, were non-existent; whether thought or action, it's all just a matter of communication. If true, then social taboos would necessarily be present mentally too, because there is no boundary between the two.

Society stops actions that would be damaging to it. If thoughts can be damaging to us, then our minds must have systems that prevent harm in the same way. Can our thoughts be damaging to us? Surely these things are mental, not physical. Before we can even think about answering this, we must set aside distress, anguish, and mental agonies, and consider them harmless, for if they are harmful, then thoughts can, obviously, be damaging.

If we partake in society then we are bound by its rules. We depend on others: for food, for shelter, for friendship, for many things. If certain thoughts stop people from behaving effectively in society, then those thoughts are damaging. There are consequences for how we act; we may be shunned, ridiculed, starved, stoned. A mechanism to limit any harmful thoughts would grow to exist, even if it is only a simple matter of learning how to conform socially to the extent that is needed, or that we are comfortable with.

Perhaps, in extreme situations, this limiting mechanism can malfunction. Our minds may inevitably make links between our thoughts and actions, and the social result. If we are learning how to behave, what if the lessons are unlearnable because we are socially punished for good thoughts and actions, or socially rewarded for bad thoughts and actions? What if our punishments or rewards are irrational and unrelated to our behaviour? If our brains are unable to comprehend the links between our actions and the social consequences, then the patterns that help us conform may become malformed; we would be trained to behave in unusual ways, all in an attempt to conform to our circumstances. Extreme thoughts such as hallucinations, delusions, paranoia, may be the result of this mechanism; not mental malfunctions, but the normal functions of a mind trained to conform to extraordinary circumstances.

Are there limits to imagination? If the brain is a machine that accepts, processes, and ejects data, then the theoretical limit is set by the amount and variety of data absorbed.

That was quite a cold, mathematical answer. Can censoring of our thoughts limit our imagination? This depends ultimately on what we express. Take two identical people, both with identical behaviour, but one with boring, tedious thoughts, and one with an extreme imagination. If they behave identically, then the imagination has had no negative, or limiting, or indeed any, effect. Only when the thoughts are expressed do the effects of the imagination become apparent, so again, the boundary between thinking and action has evaporated.

So our herald can proclaim that there are no limits to imagination except related to the amount of lovely source material we feed into our, alas limited but capacious, brains, and the limits imposed by social constraints.

"The mind of the man who dreams is fully satisfied by what happens to him," wrote André Breton[1]. This is true, but at some point we must act, and then there is always the question of social compromise.

The herald sounds his trumpet. Imagination is freed, and is happy. Even André Breton is happy because everything is elucidated. Of course, I never met him at all. He is quite dead, except in our minds.

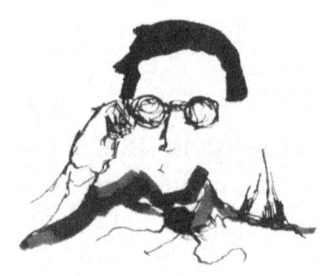

A STUDY OF SCARLET

Phantoms of the Mind

Our meandering through these smooth Orphean caves is nearly complete, but our winding path continues for the moment. This labyrinth is shaped like the wrinkles of our very brain. Amazingly, there are people here. It appears that our minds reflect our society, we are, after all, social animals.

When we meet someone new we create a phantom copy of that person that we carry in our minds. This phantom copy is stored as our reference copy of the person we know and we carry it around, among a crowd of others, all different people inside our heads. When communicating with someone, we use this reference copy to help forecast how the actual person will react.

How we feel about someone is an exact refection of how we feel about the phantom copy of the person in our heads. When we like someone, the nice feeling comes from the fact that it is part of ourselves that we like, and when we dislike someone, the pain and discomfort comes from the fact that we are disliking the part of us that is them. Friends we know well, lovers, take up more space in our heads. To suddenly dislike them causes great agony because a larger part of our brain (body, soul, universe) is taken up by them.

The more intimately we know another person, the larger and more accurate the reference copy of that person in us will be, we say that 'we know' them; it's a common expression: 'I know that person', yet we rarely analyse what this means, that we are applying the rules of abstract knowledge such as 'I know the sky is blue' to a person. We know people by degrees, and the more we know of them, the more of our brains are used to create their map, a more accurate copy of their personality in our minds. We tune to people that are similar to ourselves because this is a more efficient use of our existing brain space.

Our brains are finite in size, so the more gregarious we are, the less well we must know the individuals that we are connected to.

We can never know another person totally; even if our brain was the same size as another person's, we couldn't match it because we need some parts of our brain for ourselves. And of course, we tend to know more than one person. All of the phantom models that we hold are necessarily approximations. People with greater brain capacity can form more accurate maps of people with lesser brain capacity. Forming an accurate copy of another person is called empathy.

There are important implications for this phantom model.

Firstly, our phantoms can be realistic or unrealistic reflections of the person we are mapping. What we call misunderstandings are differences between our model of the person and their actual self. We can change our models, re-imagining how a person thinks or feels; changing, modifying, and transforming a person in our minds. These modifications happen on a daily basis. Consider our perceptions of political leaders and how accurate they are. We might make their image deliberately inaccurate, to convince ourselves that they are like us and have our best interests at heart, or to convince ourselves that they are cruel, inhuman. Racial (or any other form of) prejudice is essentially fitting a simplistic average model to someone.

Secondly, we can hold phantoms of people that do not exist. Fictional characters, imaginary friends, people in dreams; these are all examples of phantom copies of personalities that do not exist in real life.

Thirdly, we hold phantom copies of animals and inanimate objects. This in an innate ability; we give things personalities, and these are stored using the same mechanism as phantom people. Like people, our phantom objects can take up greater or lesser parts of our brains, and every emotion can be applied to them. Breaking a favourite cup can feel exactly like the death of a friend, if the size of our phantom was similar, because the mental process is identical.

By this rationale, we love and hate objects as we love and hate people. Applying feelings to objects is not less or more moral than applying feelings to people. It is a common insult that people have been 'objectified', meaning having less emotion applied to them, when objects can be 'humanised' by the same mechanism. Objectification in this context essentially means having a smaller, less accurate, phantom model applied to the person, giving them less time and attention. Naturally, that would be considered an insult, yet it is not accurate to compare this action to how we treat objects. People, objects, animals; all things are stored, thought of, felt of, in the same way.

Everything and everyone we interact with is a mental phantom in our minds, and it is our emotional interaction with these phantoms that defines our daily happiness, sadness and emotional life.

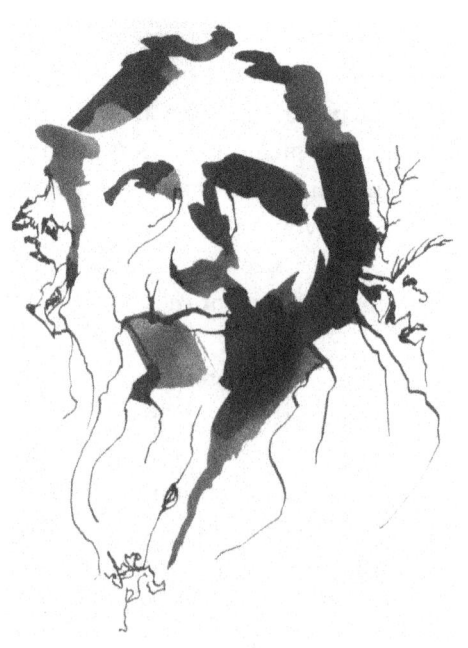

Weep! This section about the dawn of surrealism, about the mind, and a startling theory of the unconscious, is drawing to a close. Weep!

We have thoroughly attacked the art of random nonsense and, even more so, that of the ordinary, the tawdry, and the comfortable. We have clarified the role of the enigmatic and glanced upon a few golden beams that are fused into the soul-substance of great artworks.

We could stop now, but no. Dry your tears, dear traveller, for I see a distant light on the eastern horizon. Some of the rules of masterpieces could benefit from being clarifying and classifying.

Put down your trumpet and leap onto your horse. Let us charge onward.

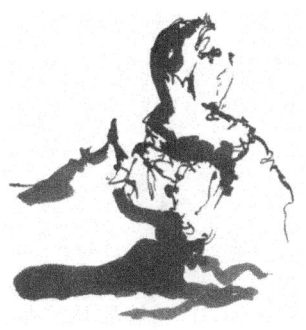

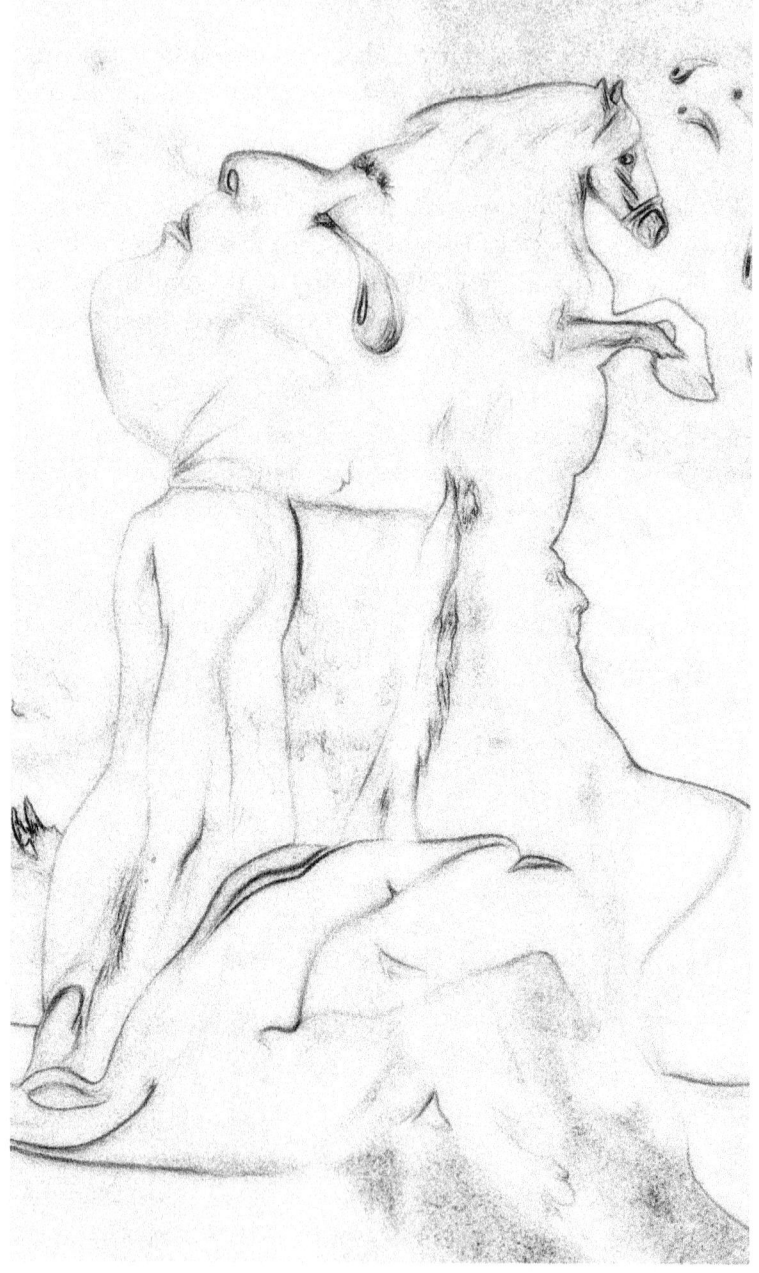

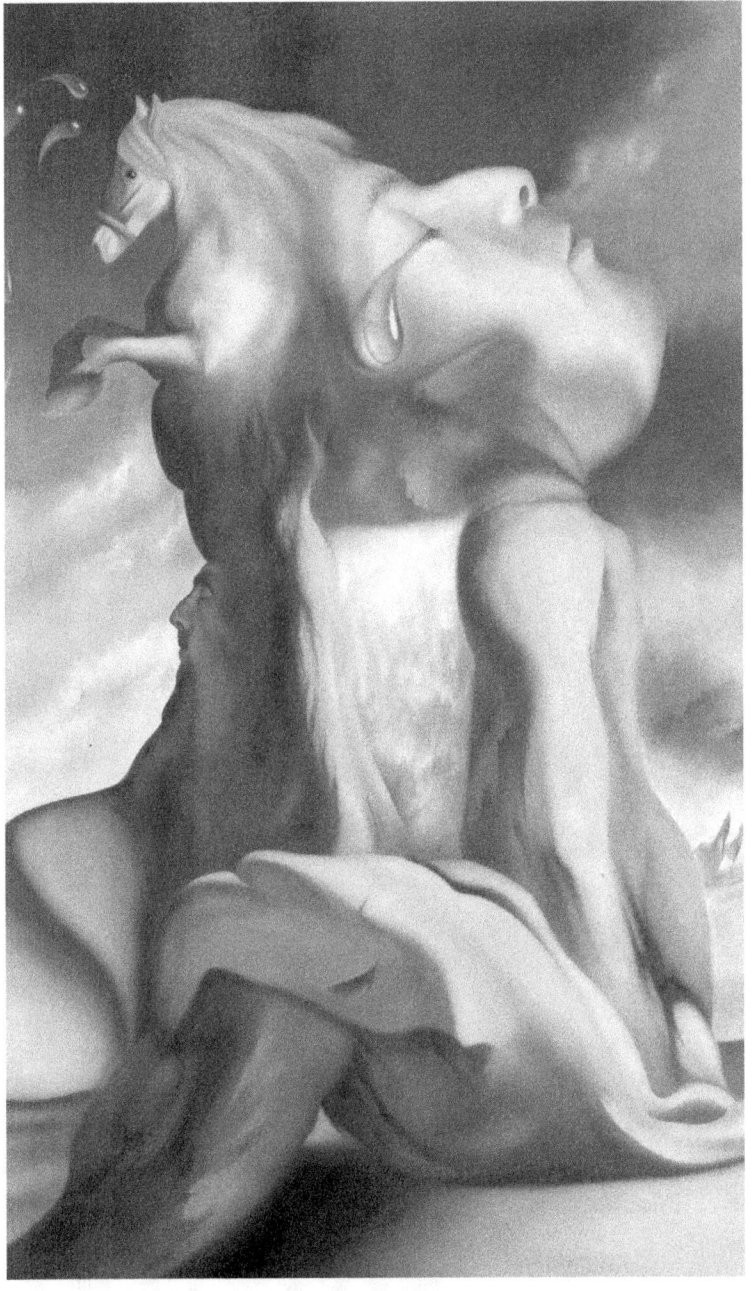

THE TOMB

21st CENTURY SURREALISM

THE TOMB

The Threshold

Now, dear traveller, before we enter the wondrous garden at the end of this book, we must enter a tomb of darkness; solemn, and wreathed in shadows and whispers. This castle is formed from the essence of Albrecht Durer's melancholy.

Art stems from solitude, ache and desire. This rocky palace-like place[1] is a sculpture of longing. It is beautiful, and powerful, and filled with every tool we need to create something from nothing. An artist creates value from nothing, it is a form of magic. Imagination and magic have been linked for centuries, because they are the same thing. What we modern humans think of as magic is a fascinating influence over others. Even now, we think of an audience as 'entranced', as 'having a spell cast over them'. The electric tendrils that emanate from an artwork are chains of desire, of longing, satisfied.

Of course, in ancient times, lawless times, where few could read and nothing was truly explained or truly known, magic was real. These powers are seen as irrelevant relics now, yet deep within all of us beats the memory of those forces, those times when magic held us all together in its web, connected us to the natural world with its delicate, invisible tendrils. In our souls we all carry memories of that time when once all things, even the rocks, were living and part of us.

Life is an extension of our thoughts. We artists must weave these thoughts into reality to share them. Our perspective of the world is unique, and we each occupy a universe filled with only our knowledge, accumulated from our personal experiences and our unique viewpoint. Our universe overlaps with those of others, so there is a consensus universe, but there are always aspects of our universe that are unique to us, or radically different from the average. It is the job of an artist to communicate these unique insights to others in a way that they can understand.

The gateway before us leads to the domain of creation and reflection. The artists' path is solitary, and then it is social. We live in an eternal cycle of retreat and advancement, of sleep and waking, of death and birth. The loneliest task of any creator is the most glorious: to explore what is new; to share new insights with a world that knows nothing of them. All artists must push boundaries, and all frontiers must be explored alone.

The entrance awaits.

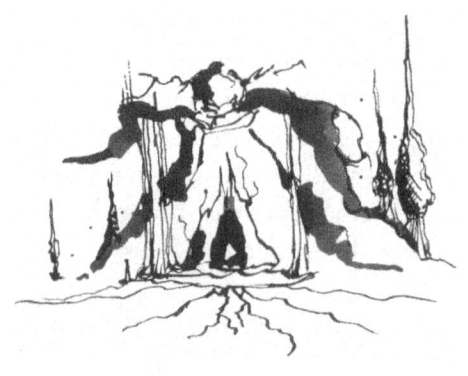

THE TOMB

Solitude

The hallway is peaceful, quiet.

"Hello?"

There is no reply. There is only a velvet blackness here. This is the soul of Melencolia Imaginativa[2], the locus of loss.

As well as our immediate senses, we have social senses and other wider tendrils of connection to the world. These are mere extensions of our personal senses. To have no contact with the outside world is sensory deprivation, a form of blindness. If you lived in a windowless cell, for example, this is apparent: you could see your hands or the walls, but nothing beyond, so as far as most of the world was concerned you would be identical to a blind person.

Just as dreams and visions bubble to the surface of our minds when we close off our senses during sleep, imagination imposes itself when we close off our social senses too. It is for this reason that creative minds tend to have solitary habits, just as visionaries have ascetic ones.

To be an artist is to be this curious mix of interested, but distant. Both of these attributes are necessary components because to engage, to open your mental eyes and release your social tentacles, is to release the energy of your current ideas and silence the more subtle voices from your inner mind.

We all have the need to express ourselves, this is as natural as thinking. It takes time and peace to access the less commonly used thoughts, and to assemble those to form new and exciting things. If we spoke and communicated constantly, every thought would be loose, flying from the surfaces of our minds, and so our conversations would focus on the same subjects, and always recent things, those things which take no effort to think about or consider. People who express things that are out of social place, things not on the current lips and minds of society, are known as 'deep', and this word reflects the depth of their mental plunges.

We need silence to think deeply; it's almost as though skimming the surface of our minds shakes up the dusty trails that lead into its dark forests. We can think and act with our surface minds with rapidity and élan, but new ideas, and counter-intuitive insights take more time for our mental librarian to access and bring to the surface for our attention.

Yet, at the same time, artists, like all things, must communicate and therefore must become social. The fact that the most creative messages grow best in the dark necessitates periods of withdrawal and periods of showcasing. So many superstars say that they are 'quiet people, really' for this reason, when often they appear to be the most flamboyant and exuberant of performers on stage. The superstar must be both extremes, but only both, never either.

THE TOMB

Now, let's sharpen our wits and light up this crystal domain with some fragments of genius. The seed of our creation is ready to be planted. Let there be lightning.

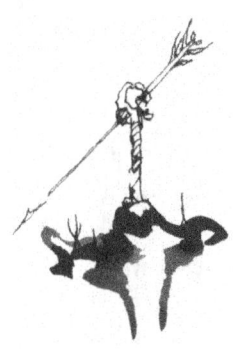

The Corridors of Creation

There are many rooms in this vast palace, and each one is designed with perfect geometry for your delight and exploration. This is the crucible of creation, our laboratory of inspiration.

As we have discovered, imagination is a seed which grows in silence. Ideas form and push towards the light of life and reality. Imagination can't be suppressed because our minds are constantly working. We think of more creative or different thoughts as imaginative, versus mundane thoughts. Everything we think can be considered a work of art, it's just that some of them are more imaginative than others.

In the thin minds of children, imaginative ideas, the most wild thoughts, are on the surface, ever flying outwards without concern of what they are, or how they affect the world. As children, we don't have many repercussions from wild thoughts and expressions of them. As adults, our creativity is generally hidden more deeply and is subjected to suspicion and scrutiny, because what we express and what we do can affect our lives or the lives of others if we have power or influence. Artists often have a special social licence to perform oddly, in contrast to politicians, for example, who can't so much as wear an unusual outfit without scrutiny.

As we know, one of the tenets of surrealism is to let ideas fly out without control. Letting these thoughts emerge while switching off our conscious minds, perhaps in something like a hypnotic trance, is called thinking 'automatically'. To be a true automatist is to be a passive observer of the images and sensations that flicker through our minds. These must bubble up gently and naturally from our inner core. This occurs by relaxing the reins of our free will. In that vulnerable and restful state we can let any deep feelings or desires manifest themselves as images, sounds, stories, and more. The hypnotic state is one of heightened awareness, created by dulling the noise of the external senses, allowing us to focus on the internal with greater clarity.

When we are dreaming our minds are doing just this. The seeds for our nocturnal adventures are scattered haphazardly. Perhaps these seeds were planted consciously if we fell asleep while thinking about something, or perhaps the seeds were sown less obviously; but it seems that some parts of our minds act as the stimulator, and other parts fill in the gaps.

In this state, it's almost as though our feelings are now guiding our senses and creating sensations, when in waking life, our feelings emerge from our senses.

It's a curious feature of biology that brain cells fire in one direction; nerve cells are, in appearance, a bit like battle-tanks with spider's legs, and their impulses fire down those tank guns, and are detected by the quivering legs of an adjoining cell. Perhaps this strange dream state is some sort of indication of a backwards motion, as though emotions emerge from experiences in our normal waking states, but experiences emerge from emotions in our dreamlike and hypnotic state.

Only a cellular tank commander can confirm this wild specu-
lation.

To create is simple: we need to expose ourselves to the max-
imum variety and quantity of information, then choose what
we want.

The unconscious is a great tool for both things. We can use
our dreams and visions as source material: to connect distant
associations, and as a filter. The unconscious, by using inkling
feelings and subtle messages, is supreme in choosing what
things will fit into our design, and what won't.

The hedges of our minds are ever moving, swirling. The most
recently absorbed information floats on the surface within our
mental arms' reach, and is the easiest to grasp at. This is often
the first out if we were to merely relax our minds. It seems to
take more time to store memories more deeply, and longer to
recall memories from the depths, too. This is perhaps one
reason why our dreams tend to focus on our most recent activ-
ities. Occasionally a distant idea will bubble up to the surface
of our minds. It is as though our minds are like the surface of
the sun, boiling with patterns that swim on the surface, but
with other shapes that emerge from deeper within its swirling
depths.

We can tune in to the quiet patterns of our dreams by simple
relaxation at any time.

If you close your eyes and stare at the blackness there, you are

training your mind's eye to see. Looking intensely at something also does this; it is for that reason why knowing how to
draw accurately is a good skill for any artist, and has always
been the measure of a visionary (note how the mystic gazes
intensely at a crystal ball). The good musician will listen and
analyse music, in an analogue of drawing, but for the ear. We
train our senses by using them; it's as simple as that. Images,
sounds, scents, and sensations are everywhere at all times, but it
is only when we actively pay attention to them that their
impact grows inside us. Without doing this, we are lazily and
voluntarily losing our valuable senses. Blindness is as much
mental as physical, and visual acuity is measured in percentage
points, not merely active and inactive. If we spend a day not
looking, we have crept, tick tick, towards blindness. The same
applies to every sense, and even our enquiring and agile minds.

When we recall memories we are exercising our brains. The
more distant those memories are, the better; recalling a distant
memory is a bit like lifting a heavier weight because we have
to cut through more layers of matted cells to get them to
twinkle into action. Even basic recollections, such as yester-
day's meals, or our dreams from last night will help our mental,
and therefore physical, fitness. We can also, read, look, listen,
and absorb any material that we might need. Anything we
expose ourselves to will remain there for some time. These
things will act as beacons and seeds, as inspiration, conscious
and unconscious. This process happens continuously, whether
we like it or not.

In the turbulent star of our minds, everything we absorb is

ultimately destined to affect us. What comes out of our minds is always a mix of what goes in.

"Now the skillful workman is very careful indeed as to what he takes into his brain-attic. He will have nothing but the tools which may help him in doing his work, but of these he has a large assortment, and all in the most perfect order. It is a mistake to think that this little room has elastic walls and can distend to any extent. Depend upon it, there comes a time when for any addition of knowledge, you forget something that you knew before. It is of the highest importance, therefore, not to have useless facts elbowing out the useful ones."

Those useful words were spoken, if they could have possibly been spoken, by Sherlock Holmes[3]. The thoughts that are nearest the door in our brain-attic are the ones that we can grasp at most easily.

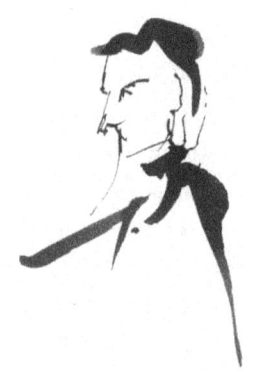

THE TOMB

The Chasm of Action

The dark path curls left and right, cutting through hard rocks of splintered granite. Our flickering fire casts a dancing light as we walk down this curious corridor. We turn a sharp corner, and touch a wall to hold on, feeling its icy wetness. The floor suddenly falls away into stark blackness, down and down to an unseen depth. Our footsteps echo around and around the vast chamber. On the opposite wall we can see our exit, a triangular hole that glows with an alluring scarlet light. We are paralysed with longing and terror.

There is a gap between inspiration and action, and it is a chasm. To some this is terrifying, and yes, creation can be because we must throw away our feelings of what is right and what is wrong. Our minds are pre-organised to know what we should be doing. These vine structures hold us together and guide us to fit in to society. To be creative, these must be bypassed and cut through. To be an artist at all is to challenge, and the more challenging the better, because to challenge is to share new information, new insight. It is easy to conform, and tempting. We can look towards other artists for help; help! We need reassurance that we are on the right path. This lonely path.

The walls are scored with initials, as guide and reassurance, the mark of Arne Saknussemm[4]:

"Descend, bold traveller, into the crater of the jökull of Snæfell, which the shadow of Scartaris tastes before the kalends of July, and you will attain the centre of the earth. I did it."

It is an irony that even the most creative artists conform within their group, but then, we must all conform to some degree because if art is communication, then rapport is part of the process. All communication is two way. We are never alone.

Yet, the path can be lonely, and there are aspects of creativity that need special encouragement. If art is a dialogue, then the ultimate encouragement will come from the audience, but when creating something, that is rarely possible because the audience can only experience the finished article. Why you, dear reader, can't even read these words as I type them on my lonely screen. The artist must have faith.

When finding a way to cross our chasm, perhaps the most important factor is our original vision. A vision can be an image, yes, the word means just that, but with an artwork in particular, the feeling is perhaps more important. It is important to know exactly the feeling, and the images, sounds and other things that stimulate it perfectly. This orb, this sculpture in your mind, will be your mental and supradimensional template for your work. It will be your endless reference point. If you are ever stuck, this sculpture will guide you to your solutions.

When this feeling is at its most powerful, it is called inspiration. It is this spark that caused your creation to exist, and a key skill to refine is holding this, remembering it, and capturing it, so that you know why you are doing something. **Why.**

This is always the most important question. When you know why, how will find its own way. When doing anything, in times of doubt, write down why you are doing it.

At times, there is no inspiration. Perhaps we lowly actors are commanded to act or create something for some vital purpose. Artists and magicians are often at the whim of sultans or other instigators, but perhaps, even when independent, there is always some sultan or some master inside us, nagging at our souls to create. To light the spark of inspiration, a deadline will help. An artificial deadline that we self-impose might help, but even for highly disciplined super-beings like us, a part of us knows that it is our deadline, and that we can simply ignore it or extend it if we really need to, so it is best not to use these. A deadline that we cannot move is always preferable, and fortu-nately we already have many of these; we all have limited free time, time before something else is due. We all have limited health; and there is death, the ultimate deadline. If you knew that you would live just one more year from today, wouldn't that deadline push you to do everything you wanted? So, there are lots of immovable deadlines that we already have at our disposal. We merely need to remind ourselves of them.

A deadline might add impetus, but what about forming that orb, that vision? Absolute certainty is always the most import-ant thing. Assemble a room of similar things, similar feelings, similar moods. Actively read, look, listen, feel the sorts of fla-vours and feelings that you desire. These objects will float and bubble in the sun-star of your mind. It is often helpful to add unexpected elements. I wrote an album of music, once, where the track titles were based entirely on random quotes. These random seeds were all that was needed to enable the process.

The menu of choices, what you want and why, will gradually swirl and coalesce into a single form, that crystal sculpture of many dimensions, of feelings and components. When we have that, the next step is to begin.

People love to finish things once they are started. Incomplete things feel messy, uncomfortable, and anxiously play upon the mind. This fragment of psychology can be used as a simple, yet powerful tool to complete anything.

The key feeling is of something being incomplete; of exactly knowing how the finished thing will look and feel, and know- ing exactly how it looks and feels now. By grasping these and feeling them powerfully, you can inspire yourself to almost effortlessly complete any task. This mix of anxiety and desire is the perfect combination to not just complete something, but to learn any new skill with incredible efficiency.

Your orb, the vision-sculpture of your complete thing, is your goal. Getting started is sometimes a barrier, but quite unexpec- tedly, you will discover that the process began at the moment you thought of it. By considering that spark of inspiration the start, the problem of making a start is instantly bypassed. From the outset, your idea was a tiny glow, a tiny fragment of a spark in the darkness, and from there it will start to grow, by gradual accretion, fragment by fragment.

The practical skills of creativity will always be secondary to those emotional ones. This is the difference between an artist and a craftsperson.

We step forwards and see the chasm retreat, our certain floor growing and supporting us with a golden bridge formed from a crystalline material. We walk along it, step by step, towards the red light, the glowing hole in the opposite wall.

When it comes to the craft of art, almost all paths involve a method. Methodology is a logical breaking down of things into steps that are mechanical and require the minimum of thought or intelligence. Most of what we think of as intelligence is fast thought. By breaking things down into rational steps, anyone can achieve anything. A computer program is exactly that, and, as our friend the chess computer will attest, a computer program can out-perform its programmer.

Some parts of any task are easier than others, and the first stage is to divide up the work into steps, work out what resources each step needs, and how long each step will take. With our immense imaginative powers we can see how the entire finished work will look before we start, and we have an idea of how much work it will be.

Accurately calculating how long a job will take is probably the most important skill of modern life. We play this game on a daily basis. The great artist has mastered this. If you are always late for appointments, take heed and make adjustments. All skills require monitoring.

Glory

Joy and love and all good things. We have emerged here, in the final chamber. These walls are skinned with gold and the choirs of immortality welcome us.

All artists live forever, because no artwork truly ends. There might be a beginning, at some sparkling inkling point, but even then, can we say that anything just appears from nothing? Once an artwork is complete, it needs filing, and storing, and promoting, and showing, and, even possibly selling, and then still promoting, and documenting, and reassessing, and rebuilding, restoring. Creation, like life, is a continuum, not an instant.

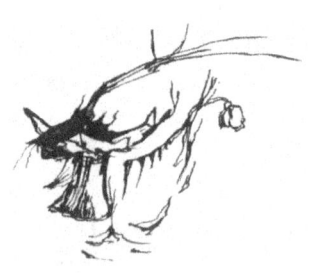

THE TOMB

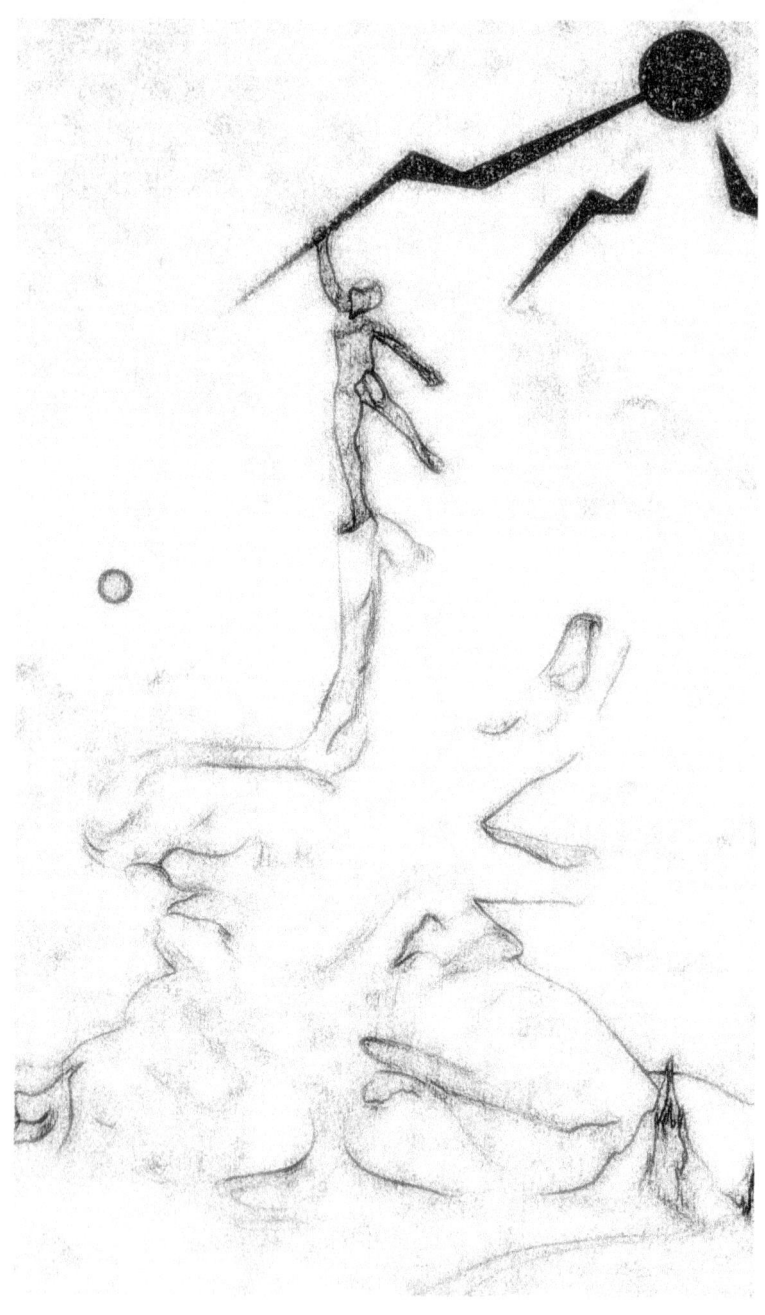

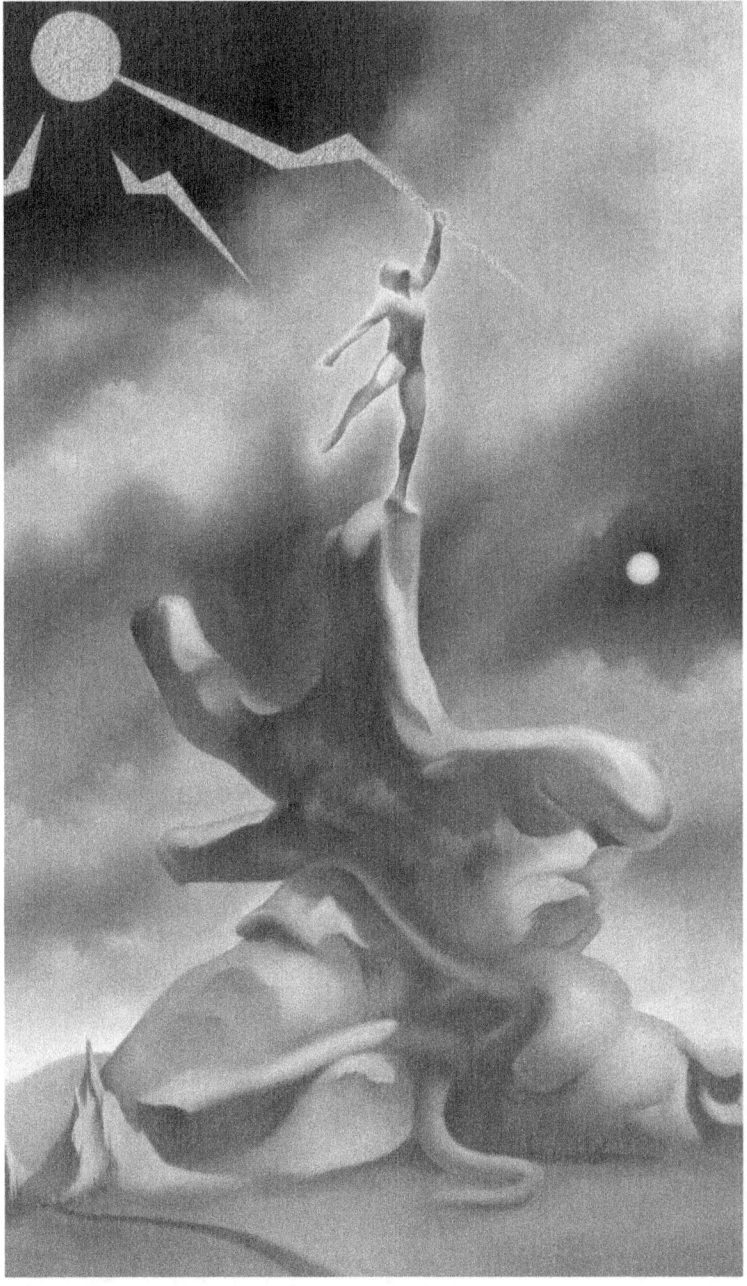

THE GARDENS OF ELYSIUM

21st CENTURY SURREALISM

THE GARDENS OF ELYSIUM

The Meadow

"VOCATUS ATQUE NON VOCATUS DEUS ADERIT"

Those words were extracted from a 16th century tome and have origins with the Oracle of Delphi. They were carved over the door of Carl Jung's house in Kusnacht and translate as "Called or not called, the god will be there."

And, yes, our heaven is here.

The sky is blue and the summer sun smiles down upon us. We lie in the long, heaven-scented grass of an infinite meadow. This is the bliss of inspiration. The air vibrates with anticipation, of activity, energy, bravery, vision. Even in this heaven, we must always be moving forwards.

The first *Manifesto of Surrealism* was a rejection of the logical and the rational, and a call to explore the untainted functioning of the mind. This led to the study and publication, with exactitude, the results of these explorations, and so became the first artistic movement with a scientific basis. It is ironic, is it not, that the most logical and practical applications were applied, uniquely, to a movement that rejected the very principle of rationality.

The results of the study led to many of the 20th century's great artworks, but the entire movement drifted away into smoke, as though in a dream itself. The results of these mental explorations were not used to formulate the broad principles of a new aesthetic theory, but instead simply considered the mental out-pourings of its adherents the end results. This is akin to Isaac Newton dramatically publishing a table of the velocity of his famous apple and considering his work complete, rather than calculating the laws that governed its motion.

This treatise is my attempt at resolving this omission, to unify a dramatic and world-shattering new theory of mind with a dramatic and world-shattering new theory of aesthetics. This claim is so bold that is has the power to shatter two worlds.

To be an artist is the ultimate profession, for it is the goal of all things to communicate as powerfully as possible, across as wide a span as possible, to as many things as possible. Even atoms aspire to be artists because their existence itself depends on this principle of intercommunication. Every day spent not doing this is a death to something unspoken to. Every unread word kills a fragment of an author just as every unwritten word kills a fragment of a reader. Every unheard note kills a fragment of a composer; so it is with silent composers, poets who don't write, and painters who don't paint. Pipe dreamers, thinkers, lazy poets – these are as effective as corpses. One measure of the success of an artist, of any being, is in the quantity of his or her output, and its variety, and its variety of destinations.

Yet, what can we create?

It is better to create anything than nothing, but some creations have more power than others. Communicating what is already known is the same as not communicating anything, so its important to communicate the unknown, different things, new things, good things! Amazing things!

Ah, the amazing. Can we ever guide the amazing? Can we quantify the fantastic? What art is, and what good art should be, is a vast topic, and, dear reader, we are about to explore it.

We stand here, in this summery field, before two elaborate gates of gold metal, with curls and swirls of infinite beauty and mystery. These gates open into five wondrous gardens, each filled with flowers and sun-scented hedges, the patterns of mystery and order; mazes cut like maps to a specific design.

Let us push open the heavy hinges to the first garden, and enter.

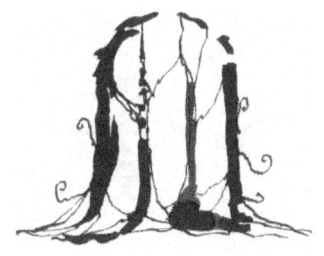

21st CENTURY SURREALISM

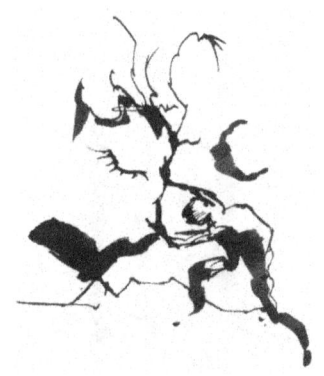

THE GARDENS OF ELYSIUM

The First Garden: Struggle

The gate is very heavy, we must push, push, push. A horn sounds the note of E♭. It is the sound of the heroic Herr Beethoven; a composer who is eternally wrestling. Beethoven had a saying: What is difficult is good.[1] These five simple words were his guide, and they pushed him to create some of the greatest music in history.

Good art is difficult to make, and the best art is extremely difficult to make.

Why?

If everyone can do something, it is common, mainstream, the median. If fewer people can do something then that act becomes more valuable. The most difficult things are the most rare, so the best art must be the result of the most difficult acts.

Of course, rarity doesn't always equate to quality; alas, unique rubbish exists, so there is more to a masterpiece than simply rarity, but that which is common or easy to create will never be considered high quality. The best things will always be rare because only a few people can make them, just as the greatest achievements will be rare because only a few people can achieve them.

Now, what is meant by difficult? There are examples of extreme toil and hardship to create something that doesn't look difficult to make, or could even have been done more easily in other ways. We could, if we wanted, paint a copy of the *Mona Lisa* with a minuscule paintbrush gripped by our perfect teeth, perhaps as we stood on one leg, and used just one laboured stroke per day for an entire century. This would be difficult, but the resulting painting wouldn't necessarily look better than an artwork painted more conventionally in a tenth of the time, so it is important that the effort expended on an artwork is made clear. That said, even in this example, the *tooth-brush one-leg century Mona Lisa* (as it will now be known as) already feels more valuable to us than the copy that took us a mere ten years.

Ideally, the difficulty in creating an artwork should clearly be evident in its results, it should simply prove its brilliance. A great artwork is instantly, viscerally, overtly great, and simply looks masterful.

However, as in our *Mona Lisa* example, an act of creation can be documented and expounded to prove the immensity of its task of creation. At this point the documentation process becomes part of the artwork, part of the story that needs to be communicated, so that process itself needs assessment. This is often used in film and television with 'making of' features; documentaries that enhance the quality of the artwork with a guide that proves its complexity. This works well in film because the act of communicating how a film was made is also a film. The overall work is more unified, and it is easy to show alongside the artwork.

There can be no exact definition of what is difficult because this is constantly changing.

A mere photograph from a century ago would have made the world gape with amazement five centuries ago. Computers can create beautiful artworks with a single click, but perhaps the first person to create the program, then click, would have made something special. Only that person would know how difficult that his or her task was, and thus how rare it was.

Rarity and difficulty are linked, which can inherently create value, but there can be some pitfalls associated with struggle. Some struggles are artificial because we might find something difficult to do that others find easy, so it's important to be aware of what can be done and what is being done. Technology drives art, and will always hold a peculiar fascination.

Technology as a tool can make things easier, so, in this garden, we might think that it harms art. Perhaps it does. Technology has been a particular driver of music over the last few decades, with new instruments and new recording techniques relentlessly pushing the medium into new territory. Can we say that music is better now than it was? Music is certainly easier to create now, and so more prolific, and cheaper, but it is also easier to sell and distribute, which is an important part of an artwork; art must be seen and shared. If it isn't shared, it might as well not exist. The purpose of art is communication.

Even with technology driven music, the most difficult music to create would be the most rare, and although that might not be the best, it is certain that the easiest, and most common creations will never be the best. Psychologically, nothing worthwhile is easy, and perhaps it is the communication of this universal feeling that is the essence of this place.

The statue in this garden is a clenched fist and it is inscribed 'PROOF!'. Proof is the key factor.

There are sinister forces and cheats at every corner. If you can cut corners, then others can too. Beware! There can be no shortcuts. If anyone can do it: if it's easy, if it's lazy, if it's common; it's bad quality work.

THE GARDENS OF ELYSIUM

21st CENTURY SURREALISM

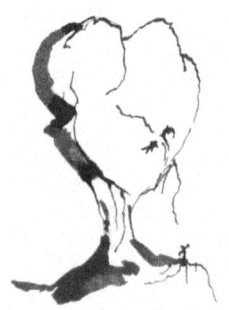

THE GARDENS OF ELYSIUM

The Second Garden: Emotion

The golden gates to this garden have a sign hanging on them, a sign carved by André Breton himself:[2]

"Let us not mince words: the marvellous is always beautiful, anything marvellous is beautiful, in fact only the marvellous is beautiful."

Art is emotional communication and the better the art is, the more powerfully it makes us feel.

Why?

If art is to do anything, it must communicate, and the more powerfully something makes us feel, the stronger the level of communication. Everything and everyone we know is part of us, and the way these parts communicate with each other in our minds is by using feelings. Feelings are a fundamental part of humanity and biological life; and perhaps the ultimate goal of art is to communicate how we feel.

We communicate feelings most effectively with those who are like us. The greater the difference between artist and audience, the more unpredictable the emotional effect. This has implications for artificial intelligences which, even today, create. It also makes inferences about animal artists, cats and monkeys and such who occasionally hit the headlines by making art and selling them to gullible people for large sums. Their paintings may exactly communicate to other animals how they feel, but the effect of animal art on humans is as unpredictable as the effect of our art on them. Of course, the gullible people probably love the entrancing effect of their new purchase, but its probably not the effect that the animal was intending; that's the crucial point.

Irrespective of any philosophy of the nature of art, emotions help us remember, and help us take notice. An artwork without emotion is liable to be ignored and forgotten.

Is it possible to create a good artwork with no emotion? No. It is impossible to create an artwork that conveys no emotion because the very context in which an audience experiences an artwork is evocative. Art is a dialogue, and it is the feelings in the audience that are present. Of course, an unfeeling audience will make any artwork emotionless. In that case, one could say that the artwork is bad or has failed, but only because art is communication; an artwork will always take two to succeed.

All artworks convey different degrees of emotion, and this will always be different for each member of its audience, but we can say as a general rule that the more emotionally powerful an artwork is, the better it is.

Emotional power is contrast; the difference between two different feelings. Rebellion, struggle and revolution are excellent forces in art for this reason. An artwork can battle against society and prevailing social feelings to become powerful, or, in the case of timeless works, contain emotional contrast within it. For an artist, as I'm sure you have always suspected, comfort is an enemy. Beware the contented artist!

Are some emotions better for art than others? It's commonly thought that happy art is somehow not as effective as sad art, but there is no reason why this should be true. All emotions are valid colours of communication, valid parts of life.

There is a particular emotional effect in economics called 'loss aversion' which indicates that the feelings of loss, at losing something, are about twice as powerful as the feelings of joy at gaining something. Perhaps, as a result of this, artworks of loss are more prevalent, and perhaps this explains why news stories of things going wrong, of loss, of disaster, are more prevalent in an open, frictionless, news system.

There can be no strict rules to emotions because they are unique to us all. These forces must simply be felt.

These Glowing Clouds

As artists, dear friends, we must evoke feelings. For reference and use, here is a menu of emotions, which you might find useful. After this we will delve a little deeper into what emotions are, and why we can never truly define them.

First, here are the 'six basic emotions' that all humans are supposed to be able to recognise in each other by their facial expressions, and so could be considered the most universal. These were compiled by Paul Ekman et al. in 1992 after a cross-cultural study: Anger, Disgust, Fear, Happiness, Sadness, Surprise.

Here is a larger list of moods, arranged to fit into one neat glance:

ecstasy, love, joy, lust, happiness, gratitude, longing, serenity, admiration, infatuation, trust, confidence, acceptance, dreaminess, fear, dread, shock, worry, torment, suspicion, unease, insecurity, awe, thrill, amazement, surprise, hope, expectation, optimism, grief, anguish, pain, sadness, dejection, apathy, loneliness, relief, loathing, hate, disgust, shame, remorse, disapproval, boredom, anger, contempt, jealousy, envy, passion, annoyance, frustration, zeal, anticipation, enthusiasm, vigilance, anxiety, bewilderment.

Those are mere words, seeds for inspiration. One of our posits is that emotions should be felt and can't be fully rationally described; we can only describe a feeling with what causes it. If, as we recall our little chess computer friend, these feelings emerge from the way our minds process what we sense, then this is quite understandable. We can explain words and letters and grammar, for example, but if we were faced with only the feeling we get after reading a great novel, then try to explain that feeling without using the words, it would be an impossible task. Feelings flow from one-way streets. Emotions are like smoke clouds that fuzz around the hard branches of trees of logic; they can't be squished back into the branches, but they will naturally, and unavoidably, form and glow around them.

It is ironic then, that artists need to do this; take a feeling and initiate it by stimulating the senses. For now, we will write this point down on a piece of paper, roll it up, and put it into a small bottle of blue glass. Remember to cork it.

As feeling creatures, we are constantly faced with experiencing the result of our personal brain logic, all triggered by various senses; from both the real world and from our thoughts and memories. We can try to link those senses with the feelings, and might have some success; eating ice cream might make us feel happy, but that doesn't prove that ice cream is linked to happiness in a fundamental way. There are too many variables involved in feelings to pin them all down, the combinations are vast because everything we experience is part of the equation; yes, speaks the god-like voice; the entire universe affects how we feel. Is it not so that a distant twinkling star can make us feel awed? Even the thought of it can make us feel dreamy. See how feelings have been created from these tiny fragments.

More than this, feelings are much more than bold and obvious things like happiness, love, anger, and these powerful, passionate fires. We are aglow with feelings at every level: the feeling of being on the second step of a ladder rather than the first, the feeling that there is a porcelain cat on the oaken fireplace, the feeling that the sky outside might have the flavour of blackcurrants. These are valid emotions. You may have just felt them, which proves it. None of these gentle things would be considered fundamental human feelings.

We are constantly beset with these inklings at every moment.

Emotions can never be taxonomically catalogued or classified in the way that, for example, elements in the periodic table are classified, because there are too many variables, and some of those variables are unique to each individual. However, if our minds share common traits, and similar senses stimulate similar emotions, then we can share them. We can use this fact to make general rules and say things like what we call 'happiness' feels like this, this recognisable glow that we may recognise in future.

Each person, and each animal, and even each chess computer, feels in a different way. What one person identifies as 'feeling happy' is not exactly what another person does, and it is again different to the feeling an animal feels; although it may be more or less similar based on the greater or lesser similarities of our minds, our senses, and our experiences.

Words that describe emotions are labels of convenience.

Animals may feel emotions so differently to us that to apply human words to them might be misleading, but they might be close enough to be useful. We can see a happy little dog, and feel confident that it's feeling something that we can identify with, but few people would say that they can detect angst or melancholy in a distant squirrel. We could say that our friend the chess computer feels nervous if he (it is now a him) suspects his opponent is going to put his king in 'check', but this nervousness isn't really like the nervousness that we humans would feel. It's a unique emotion that only another chess computer would really feel and understand. Of course, being computers, and therefore identical, two chess computers like this have the capacity for greater empathy between them than people have. Isn't this unexpected? That computers could be more empathic than people.

The very joy of works of art is that they can evoke feelings that can be experienced only by experiencing the art. Like that great novel we talked about: if we can read it, we don't have to make other people feel the feeling, we just have to let them read it too, or tell them about it, knowing that we'll tell it slightly differently, and give them a slightly different experience of the story.

Let us uncork that little blue bottle and take out the little roll of paper. Ah, yes. As artists we must toy with any senses we choose to stimulate feelings. Thus, we need to be masters of sensual stimulation and its evocative effects.

We do this by creating something, experiencing it, and seeing how it makes us feel, then hoping that other people will feel the same. People who are similar to us will be affected in a similar way to us. People who are different from us won't be.

Fortunately, all humans are pretty similar, and even artificial intelligences will probably have peers. At least here, if our theory is correct, we have shown that they too will have feelings.

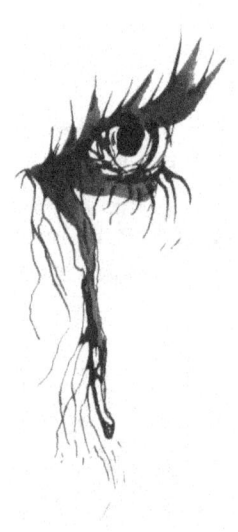

THE GARDENS OF ELYSIUM

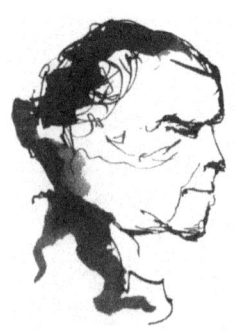

THE GARDENS OF ELYSIUM

The Third Garden: Information

Ah, the third garden. The gates here are formed of intricate curls and whirls, filled with numbers and letters and a vast panoply of symbols. We could spend all day just looking at them, but no, we must push on and enter this amazing maze of fantastic topiary. Everything here is rich; rich and complex, like life.

The best art is rich in information content. The more information an artwork contains, the better.

Why?

Just as the goal of life is the transmission of information, so this is the purpose of art. The existence of things depends on one's knowledge of things, which depends on the transmission of knowledge, therefore the greater the quantity of information transmitted, the greater the artwork.

But, surely, size isn't everything. Is it really the case that a four hour Wagner opera, for example, complete with its pretty costumes and set designs, is better art than a three minute pop record by The Beatles? These are very different entities. Can you even say that a four minute pop record by The Beatles is better than one of three minutes?

Perhaps the scale of an opera can lead us to experience awe or despair in a way that a three minute pop song cannot, but perhaps that's just a factor of the medium. A two hour film might be able to produce the same gamut of emotions as a three hour film. Let's consider two artworks that were equally difficult to create, and that we feel equally strongly about, yet one is larger and more complex than the other; can we really say the larger one is a better work of art than the smaller? Whole art genres, such as Minimalism, are affected by this. Do these result in worse art than, for example, a complex genre like Art Nouveau or Abstract Expressionism?

Perhaps size isn't the right thing to consider; our initial premise was quantity of information. Is a simple three minute piece of music better than a complex three minute piece? Or a complex painting better than a flat band of colour?

The more information, the more depth, an artwork has, the more it takes an audience to absorb. A complex artwork offers more. The audience can experience it on a superficial level; you may casually listen to Beethoven's Ninth Symphony or casually gaze at Hieronymous Bosch's *The Garden of Earthly Delights*, but you can spend more time on those works and so gain more from them. An artwork is a dialogue, and an artwork with more information to give allows the audience to give too, which leads to a richer and more satisfying experience. The more we give, the better we feel. Simplicity is less satisfying than complexity.

Quantity of information doesn't always correlate to size, many small works can be rich in information, detail, and message. Information is provided by contrast, even in computing this is the contrast between zero and one. Contrast demands extremes of variety, so the ideal artist has a infinite range of knowledge, is a master of all media and interests, and has any skill from an infinity of skills at his or her disposal. The most dense information demands the highest contrast, the widest range of numbers, of colours, of timbre, of loudness.

This relates to emotional power, which is also created by contrast. There may be scientific rules to information quantity, but there are also human and emotional ones. Information can be emotional or intellectual, and each can affect the power of the other; ideally each will complement and enhance each other.

Emotions can change with the flow of social attitudes, and the extremely fickle mood of the audience, whereas intellectual information can endure for much longer. For this reason, immortal masterpieces contain a lot of their own information, rather than relying on contemporaneous, transient, social attitudes or knowledge.

Digitisation

The use of digital technology in creativity has increased steadily since around 1980, and in general its use has resulted in lazy, generic art that is low in content, low in emotional quality, and, because of all of these factors, value.

This is a bit of harsh statement, I mean, even this very book, an object of supreme beauty, and perhaps even... love, is created using a computer. However, computers have already had a massive impact on humanity and culture, and there is something about music from the pre-digital era, the nineteen-seventies and earlier, that oozed feeling and artistry compared to the music in subsequent decades. We can fondly remember dramatic television themes like the *Weekend World* theme, the romance of *The Clangers*, the jazzy evocations of *The Odd Couple*. Feeling in modern music has been all but assassinated, especially in what we might call 'graphic' music; music created in large quantities for the practical purposes of television and advertising.

In the olden days, the word graphics meant practical rather than fine (fine means arty, and/or useless and impractical) art. The term stuck to refer to computer graphics, which perhaps indicates that computers were initially a creation tool to help with the mass production of, well, graphics; packaging, advertising, posters, and that sort of thing. Few people would want to go back to the days of hand painting the written credits on a film.

We, though, are fancy fine (fine means arty and/or aesthetically and philosophically astute) artists, and as computers continue their inevitable replacement of human and animal functions, it's important to be aware of the effects of digital creation methods upon that which is created.

Digitisation is the act of converting information into numbers, whether text, sounds, pictures, or anything else. In all cases, except when actually recording lists of numbers, some information is destroyed by digitisation because the rough and lumpy real world is averaged out; quantised and quantified.

This effect isn't always negative; a major benefit of digitisation is to make things neater and more orderly. It's for this reason why this book works better when type-written rather than hand written. A hand written copy might be more expressive and rich in extra information, but it would be less neat and perhaps more difficult to read, as well as being massively more work to create, and with far less control over the process. A hand written copy would be more valuable, however, because it would be unique, more expressive, and have required more skill.

A second reason for digitisation is that it makes creating an exact copy possible. Many great paintings of the past now exist as digital images of the original work. Three-hundred pixels per inch is currently the standard level of quality when digitising images (for readers in the distant future, an inch was an archaic measurement based on the size of a body part of a long forgotten monarch. Embarrassed by the illogic of this measurement, Americans try to pin the use, and thus the name, of these units upon the English, who have long since rejected them). Of course, an oil painting in real life has a far higher resolution than this; one dot per molecule of linseed oil, which is about 1.5nm in diameter. If we make some allowances for other binders and pigments, this equates to a resolution of around 4 billion dots per inch, which means that well over 99.9999% of even basic visual information is lost when an oil painting is scanned, and of course, a painting is far more than its mere flat visible surface, we have depth, texture, and a range of colours that a digital scanner cannot exactly replicate. The joy of pigments is that each one has a unique and complex spectrum.

When a digital image is printed, more information is added back (phew), far more than the simple list of numbers that define the image. Each printed image is packed with feelings and sensations; consider the thick, plasticy feel of a Polaroid photograph, the moth-wing softness of a delicate sheet of paper, the scent of the page, the exact hue and shine of the ink, and how the particles are scattered. All of these attributes affect how we perceive a printed image.

Of course, this loss of information isn't disastrous. Humans are exceptionally good at filling in missing pieces; most people wouldn't be able to tell the difference between a printed copy and a real life painting, or a digital sound recording and its live source, and, as with our example, we inevitably add new information when the artwork is converted back into the real world where the audience live.

It is important to note, however, that destroying information will always reduce the limits of emotional power, because less information will inevitably affect its gamut to some extent; its range, its contrast, and therefore its drama, and that is almost always detrimental to an artwork. The quantity and variety of information available to us when working solely in a digital realm is minuscule compared to the range available in real life.

The simplicity of information in a digital work equates to a loss of expressive power, and as a result, digital works can be cold; too mechanical, too regular. This is perhaps most apparent in music, where digital sequencers use regular timing and regular volume levels. This perfect regularity is an extreme form of digitisation, and lacks expression because it lacks variety.

Cold regularity can be useful as a contrast for natural organic rhythms and emotions, but even in such circumstances, the cold emotionlessness of a regular rhythm always appears bright, jarring, and unnatural, compared to an organic performance, because it is very quantised, very low in information content.

By comparison, the power of classical music comes from the fact that each player is a human being, expressing his or her own feeling. Each performer in the orchestra is filled with abilities, memories, sensations, and all combine additively to bring a vast quantity of information into a large, orchestral performance. A single electronic instrument could never match this depth and variety on a pure informational level.

It is variety that conveys information, not regularity, because information is a contrast between two things. It is the regularity of digital information that harms its expression. When creating digitally there is more emphasis on the artist to add information and add feeling, and this can be achieved by breaking up the regularity and uniformity of the work; battling against the very two forces that digitisation imposes upon it.

The greatest benefits of using computer technology for creation are control over the process, the ability to copy and store work, the ability to process information in complex ways, and ease of use.

Computers perform many functions far more efficiently than humans, and it is this efficiency and convenience that is their greatest strength. Computers store and transmit information more securely than biological life, and perhaps it is inevitable that the functions of people and animals will gradually be supplanted by such machines, but let's be aware of how crude and exceptionally simplistic computers are compared to biological life. This is true in 2018 and might be so for many centuries. Our biology contains four billion years worth of data.

The new will always seem alluring and amazing, but the worthwhile is never easy. Value will always relate to individual effort. Every tool must be used to the best of its ability. When wood carving, a chainsaw is not worse than a hand chisel, but its important to remain diligent and aware of the strengths, weaknesses, and limitations of any new technology.

THE GARDENS OF ELYSIUM

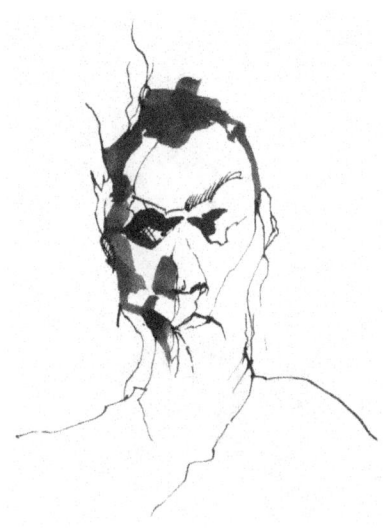

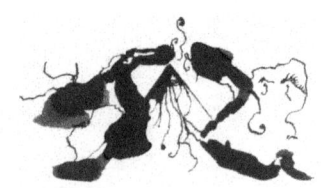

THE GARDENS OF ELYSIUM

The Fourth Garden: Enigma

It's time to enter the fourth garden. This one is dim, and lit by a curious blue light that shimmers as though its world is submerged beneath an airless ocean. Its hedge walls are cut into passages that run up and down in uneven rows. Strange, ghostly people float along the corridors of this twisted maze.

There is a fifth dimension beyond that which is known to man. Four repeating notes sing, G#, A, G#, E. It is the theme to an ancient television programme called *The Twilight Zone*. Four notes synonymous with the mysterious and the uncanny.

An enigmatic quality is important in art because the unresolvable equates to infinity. As we've explored with great élan earlier in the section about the irrational, feelings are partially kept alive by not being acknowledged, and so understanding our worries helps them go away, as though the child-like part of our brains needs to be reassured by the clever, grown-up part. The emotional power of a message depends partly on a lack of comprehension, so the enigmatic, that which can not be resolved, has the power to capture a feeling in a loop, forever. The mysterious in an artwork will make us think about it, and if the puzzle is unresolvable then we can ponder it forever, gaining an infinite amount from it. This is one of the most powerful contributions to art made by surrealism. Before the existence of surrealist artworks, symbols in art were added deliberately to convey meaning, never to sow confusion.

But is the enigmatic confusing?

The ideal enigma asks questions of the audience, it is alluring, but unresolvable. Like π, its beauty extends forever. There can be intellectual enigmas and emotional ones. People need resolution and answers, and when enticed, our minds will work ceaselessly to provide the answer.

An important question for artists is if something is unknowable, how can it be conceived and created?

An enigma, like any puzzle, must be enticing and unresolvable, but not frustratingly so. The beauty and allure of the enigma must be endlessly rewarding.

As far as the creation of enigmas is concerned, they exist in a dimension as vast as space, and as timeless as infinity. It is the middle ground between light and shadow, between science and superstition, and it lies between the pit of man's fears and the summit of his knowledge. This is the dimension of imagination.[3]

THE GARDENS OF ELYSIUM

The Chamber of Two Realities

Perhaps one of the most inspiring parts of the first surrealist manifesto was an extract of a small prose-poem that André Breton included from *Nord-Sud: Revue Littéraire*, an avant-garde magazine which ran to sixteen issues and was published in 1917 and 1918. The first surrealists were mainly writers, and many of them, including Breton, contributed to Nord-Sud which was edited by Pierre Reverdy. Issue 13 from March 1918 opens with these words by Monsieur Reverdy. I have re-translated the work and retained the bold emphasis present in the original French. It's entitled *L'Image*:

"The image is a pure creation of the mind. It cannot be born from a comparison, but the reconciliation of two realities more or less distant. The more distant and accurate the relation between the two realities, the stronger the image will be - the more emotional power and poetic reality.

Two realities that have no connection cannot be brought together usefully. No image is created. Two opposing realities have no connection. They oppose each other. We rarely get strength from this opposition.

An image is not strong because it is **brutal** or **fantastic** - but because the association of ideas is distant and true. The result obtained immediately checks the correctness of the association.

Analogy is a means of creation - It is a **resemblance of relations**; however, the nature of these relationships depends on the strength or weakness of the created image.

What is great is not the picture - but the emotion it provokes; it is on this last point that the greatness of an image is measured.

The emotion thus provoked is pure, poetically, because it was born outside of any imitation, of any evocation, of any comparison.

There is the surprise and the joy of being in front of a new thing.

We do not create an image by comparing two disproportionate realities. On the contrary, we create a strong, new image for the mind, by bringing close, without comparison, two distant realities of which the **mind alone** has grasped the relationship."

It's notable that Breton only included the first paragraph, excluding the part about images that are not connected being ineffective. It's tempting to think that André, the Dadaist revolutionary, didn't mind combining random unconnected things. Let us perish that thought.

There are lots of gems in *L'Image* that are as valid for art now as they were a century ago. The first is the effect of contrast; a greater contrast creates greater power. Contrast has a relationship to information because a scale of some sort is needed to define it, that's why things have to be related, but distant. The more distant the better. The contrast between one candle and three candles is small, the contrast between one candle and a bonfire is big; but they are both fires. There is no contrast between the planet Mercury and a hippopotamus because they are not related. Things don't have to be closely related, but there has to be some sort of connection that we can at least possibly understand.

Another truth (if I can use that bold word) we can take from Pierre's prose-poem is that in a creative work the power of the emotion, and its truth, its authenticity, its poetic reality, are the important factors.

And finally, that connecting things with no relation doesn't produce good results. Combining any old thing creates chaos. Information is always a mix of order and chaos, and aesthetics is about balancing these forces.

L'Image is about the value of hidden connections. Those will naturally form a balance of chaos and order, with a sprinkling of beneficial enigmatic qualities.

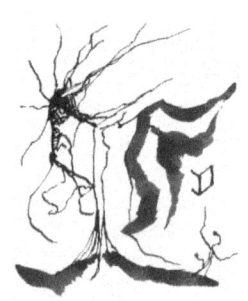

The Fifth Garden: Structure

And so we wend and wander into the final garden, a pentacle of perfect mathematical order.

A good artwork has a structure, it is more than a haphazard arrangement.

Why?

Perhaps this part is more about mere aesthetics than fundamentals. People like symmetry, for example. Does this mean that a symmetrical artwork is better than an asymmetrical one?

Generally, yes. We are making art for people, after all, and certain attributes, such as our need to seek and resolve patterns, are an inherent part of how our minds and lives work. The aim of a structural form is to impose a form of order and neatness onto the emotional and informational outpourings of the artist; it is a way of adding some order to what would otherwise be chaos. We are familiar with structures in poetry, lengths and syllables of lines. Drama has an opening, a development, a resolution. Classical music has lots of structural forms, and pop music is as structured as Victorian poetry. If structure was unimportant, these forms would not have evolved, so why do they exist, and are some structures better than others?

If I could resolve those questions I would be some sort of magician, solving those questions in one page, one page of part five of a structurally perfect book; in two halves of flowing feeling and inspirational wonder, then five distinct sections of practical formulation. The same typeface and letter size is used throughout this page, when using a different font per word would have conveyed more information, and even more feeling.

Aesthetics is the art of balancing the forces of a free imagina-tion and the expectation of an audience, it is a way for the artist to impose some sort of control over the dialogue between his or her work, and how it is absorbed by the audience. The balance is constantly shifting with trends and the tastes of an audience, and there are elements of cultural feedback; people like what is new, but not too new. It is for these reasons that structures are often loose guidelines. Art that is too structured, too orderly, too neat, is as bad as art that is too unstructured, too chaotic, too messy. This is because the balance of order and disorder is directly related to the quantity of emotional and intellectual information that can be transmitted; art with the right balance is more powerful because it conveys and expresses more.

All forms involve some sort of repetition within a pattern. When the artist and audience are familiar with a form, it can give the artist the ability to control levels of expectation and the unexpected. As an audience, we can expect what is coming next, and it is pleasant when our expectations are rewarded. When repetition is too similar, the work is simplistic and could be boring. When repetition is too different, or none existent, it can be too chaotic, confusing and demand too much attention from the audience.

Information is conveyed by balancing the forces of identical and opposite. The information is contained in the difference between similar structures; similar images, similar sounds, similar words.

Order and chaos are fundamental opposing forces in the universe. It would take a book and a lifetime, and at least some qualifications, one imagines, to prove this, but, based purely on my intuitive belief (and a few hints from the laws of thermodynamics), order leaks into chaos; and information is a mix of both. Pure order, and pure chaos, contain no information. As such, the most information is present in a fifty-fifty mix, which is why chaotic elderly minds and bodies have similar abilities to ordered young minds and bodies. A ten year old child has similar abilities to a ninety year old adult, and the most able age for a human is therefore around fifty. Feel free to test this by calculating the average age of every world leader, executive, and able human.

Let's explore an example. I will use the form of a limerick, which as I'm sure you are aware is a five line poem with the rhyming structure of AABBA. Here is a limerick with a lots of similarity and, as such, is low in information content:

There once was a man who rolled over,
and over and over and over,
and over and over,
and over and over,
and over and over and over.

This limerick is overtly simple; so simple that its structure is reduced to an AAAAA rhyming scheme, and more than that, all of the so-called rhyming words are identical. We could add more information by adding more variety to the language and the punctuation, adding a little more disorder and unexpectedness to the result, and thus creating more richness:

He was looking for comets for months,
and he used his computers for hunts,
but at midnight (about),
all the power ran out,
and he missed two that both came at once.

More punctuation can add informational richness! (please note the deliberate nature of that last exclamation mark, a symbol which is something of a taboo in contemporary literature). As a final example we could add so much information that the rhyming structure collapses to create a chaotic result:

Constable Isolde Fry,
lived on yonder Blue-beard island,
beset with many troubles,
such as disqeor mngow.
Je t'aime... moi non plus.

Would you say that the third poem is more information rich than the second, or merely more chaotic? Too much chaos can destroy information; emotional and intellectual. We could make it more ordered by making the bizarre 'disqeor mngow' actual words, perhaps ending with a word that rhymed with troubles, pulling it back a little towards the intended structure.

Art is a dialogue and the aspect of control is one of accord, not one-sidedness. This is one reason why similar forms proliferate. A sonnet form, for example, is a nice structure, and using it can help a poem because there are other sonnets to compare it with. When the reader is familiar with sonnets, each one shines with its variety within the form, rather than appearing starkly disjointed or too new.

Some media can impose new structures. Mike Oldfield's *Tubular Bells*, the original long-playing record from 1972, is effectively a symphony in two movements of twenty-or-so minutes. That form proliferated in the nineteen-seventies as a consequence of the medium. Due to vinyl, many rock or progressive albums appeared that were effectively symphonies with two or four movements of around twenty minutes.

Structural forms in visual art are limited and practically non existent today, one exception being the triptych as descended from altar-pieces, which in turn was developed for practical rather than aesthetic purposes. Francis Bacon comes to mind as a notable pioneer to break this form into an aesthetic secular setting. Painting and drawing series are now common, but these are very weak as structures, being little more than lists, a visual equivalent of our AAAAA poem. Installations and art exhibitions attempt to create large scale, though non-standardised, structures of visual artworks by creating spaces that try to manage the flow of the audience, to regulate and impose some sort of control over the final effect.

When working in structures, the best art expresses the whole in each part, such that if it could be sliced into fragments, each fragment would echo the whole feeling and concept, like a fragment of holographic paper, which, as I'm sure you are aware, shows the whole image in each particle.

And now, in sadness, we must disassemble the scaffolding of this book. Rod by rod, pipe by pipe, bolt by bolt. Down the ladders of our happiness we carry our frameworks.

THE GARDENS OF ELYSIUM

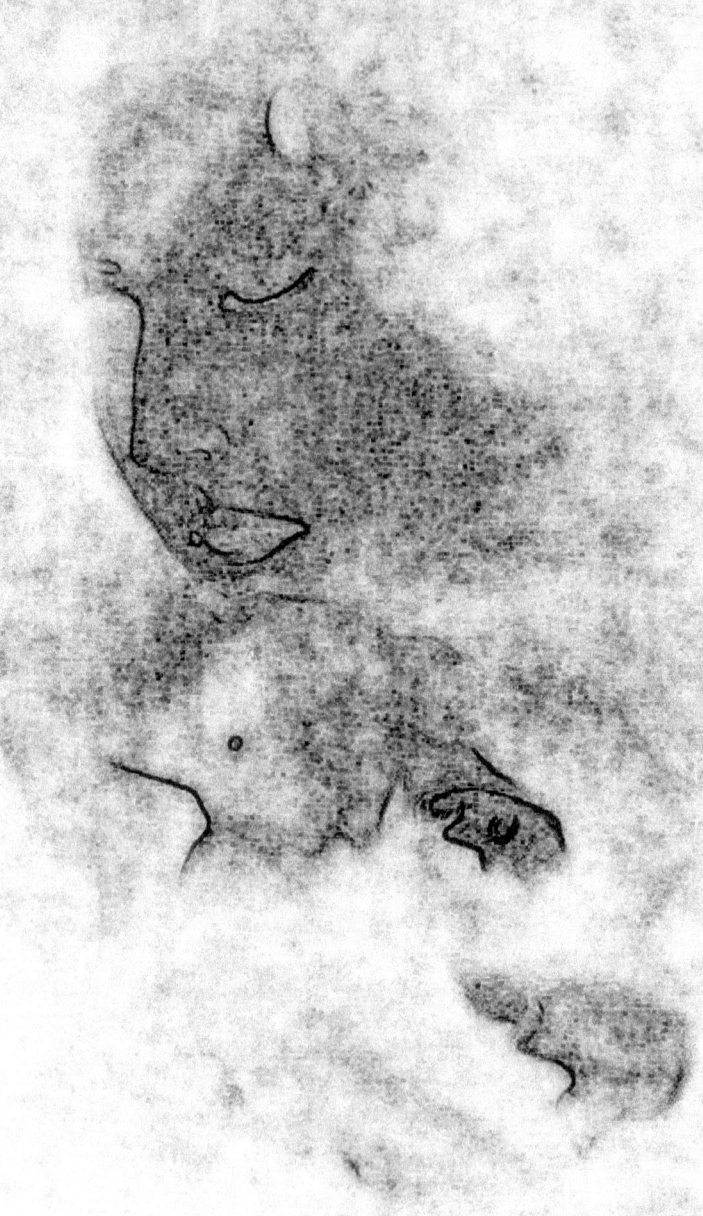

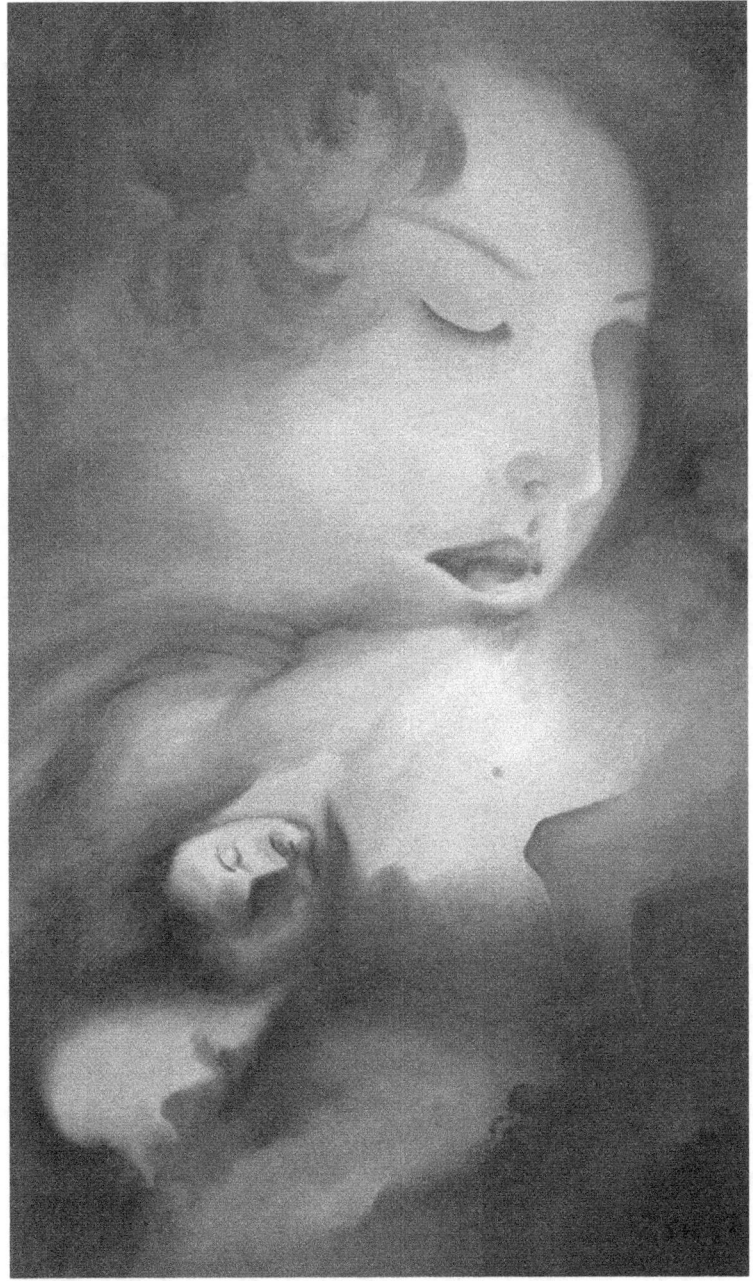

THE BOUNDLESS OCEAN

21st CENTURY SURREALISM

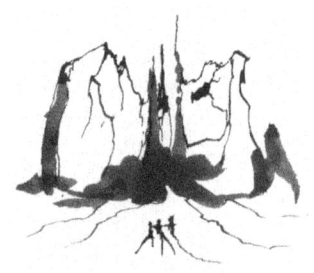

THE BOUNDLESS OCEAN

21st Century Art

The sound of the sea hisses over this island shore. We sit on the beach, vast and cold, our straggled black hair matted with sand and the rain of our tears. Our hands rake though the grit, for our time is nearly over.

I wrote this book to set down some of my personal artistic principles, and make the case for why imaginative, non-conformist art is better art than tedious art with conformist emotion.

What is art? The good art espoused here. 'Decorative Art', loathed by every artist, was herein defined so that it can be killed. Let the quaint landscapes and animal portraits that have dominated our daily eyes for the last century, die. Of course, nobody would weep.

If the history of art tells us anything, if the history of science does, it's that discoveries never end, and that new, vast worlds are always unexpected. I would imagine that in 1840, visual artists had considered their art refined to the ultimate degree, yet it was merely the start of what we call Modern Art, due to that feared invention, photography.

Now we stand on the cusp of a new dawn. The Internet marked the start of a new epoch for humanity. What makes people different from animals is that we can learn and teach. Chimpanzees can learn skills, such as breaking a nut with a tool for example, by watching other chimps, but if that chain is broken, the knowledge is lost, and a chimp must become an inventor again to relearn a skill that his or her countless forbears had invented countless times. Humans did this at first, but eventually, information stuck. Speech was developed, and stories could be passed on, and knowledge could be passed on, down the generations, and to other tribes. This was the first epoch of intelligent life. Written language was the next great leap, then printing which led to mass literacy, then electric communication which permitted the instant conveyance of the latest ideas, and now the Internet; allowing global collaboration, and access to the best knowledge and latest information in the world, instantly.

Humanity can communicate more efficiently than ever in history, and this inevitable trend will continue into a new era of non-biological intelligence, for life preserves and transmits information biologically, humanity preserves and transmits information more securely with writing and machines, and machines that can preserve and transmit information, yet better, and will surely prove themselves more efficient at this, at least, than we animals.

The Internet epoch has changed, and will change, humanity forever. It will change art too. The peaks of the exceptional humans of the past are now sanded smooth by waves of people, vast numbers of great people who can now share ideas instantly. This is the age of the genius, which makes it harder for individuals to excel; but being exceptional was never easy.

Communication is the goal of all things, and art is the ideal of communication. An artist can change the world more effect-ively than any politician. Marcus Aurelius, philosopher, Roman Emperor, is the most well known man of the 2nd century, and only because of his famous *Meditations*. His military victories and political losses are now unimportant. The aristocrats of Ludwig van Beethoven's era are remembered most commonly when their names appear in the titles of that composer's work.

I was careful in this book not to limit art to a specific medium; creativity must be untrammelled, and power and depth comes from reaching across the widest bounds. Each medium is dif-ferent, and charged with unique magic. The philosophy here indicates that every medium can generate every emotion. So let fire be released! Let alchemy begin! We stand at the dawn of a new Renaissance, and the new artist must be master of all media. The foaming sea, that first swirled in vortex when all peoples connected using computers, is subsiding. This sea is daunting, and vast, always varied, but never apathetic.

The palette is set, and now it is time to explore it, to use it to lighten up the great darkness that pervades contemporary soci-ety. As machines replace each of our functions, to create and to love art will probably be our destiny as a species.

Marcus speaks: "No, you do not have thousands of years to live. Urgency is upon you. While you live, while you can, become good."[1]

Onward.

NOTES

THE MYSTERIOUS ISLAND

1. The language and style of this section is an homage to the proto-surrealist work *Chants de Maldoror* by the Comte de Lautréamont (Isidore Ducasse).
2. A character in the play *Abigail's Party,* Mike Leigh et al. (1977). Part of the play debates the merits of the fantasy painting *The Wings of Love* by Stephen Pearson.

A STUDY OF SCARLET

1. André Breton, *Manifesto of Surrealism.*
2. It is shaped like a crucifix.
3. "(Knut Hamsum ascribes this sort of revelation to which I had been subjected as deriving from hunger, and he may not be wrong. (The fact is I did not eat every day during that period of my life). Most certainly the manifestations that he describes in these terms are clearly the same" - André Breton, *Manifesto of Surrealism*, preface.
4. Shakespeare, *The Tempest*, Act IV Scene 1.

THE TOMB

1. This word combination is an homage to David Bowie, *Glass Spider* (1987).
2. The full name of the print by Dürer known popularly today as *Melancholy*, or more correctly, *Melencolia I.* The original form of spelling may be deliberate rather than any correct historical spelling of melancholia.
3. Arthur Conan Doyle, *A Study in Scarlet.*
4. Jules Verne, *Journey to the Centre of the Earth.*

THE GARDENS OF ELYSIUM

1. In a letter of 9 January 1817 to Anton Steiner, Beethoven writes: "... for he will think that difficult is a relative term, e.g. what seems difficult to one person will seem easy to another, and that therefore the term has no precise meaning whatever. But ... this term has a very precise meaning, for what is difficult is also beautiful, good, great, and so forth. Hence everyone will realise that this is the most lavish praise that can be bestowed, since what is difficult makes one sweat." - In this case, this was a rebuke to a criticism that his works were too difficult to play. The excellent *Beethoven: Anguish and Triumph* by Jan Swafford makes a better case for the phrase 'What is difficult is good' being part of Beethoven's personal philosophy.

2. André Breton, *Manifesto of Surrealism*. The more common American translation uses the spelling 'marvelous'.
3. *The Twilight Zone* (1959).

THE BOUNDLESS OCEAN

1. Marcus Aurelius, *Meditations*, Book 4 No. 17.

Illustrations

Cover
God Being Killed By Theists And Atheists (2012)
Oil on M.D.F. panel, 222x222mm

Back Cover
The Paranoid Schizophrenia of Richard Dadd (2012)
Oil on M.D.F. panel, 400x400mm

Colophon
Magic Square from Melencolia I, Albrecht Dürer (1514)
Engraving, 240x188mm

Mysterious Island
The Last Madonna (2017)
Oil on M.D.F. panel, 222x222mm

A Study of Scarlet
God Being Killed By Theists And Atheists (2012)
Oil on M.D.F. panel, 222x222mm

The Tomb
Abandoning Someone Who Was A Friend To Me When I Had None (2010)
Oil on canvas, 222x222mm

The Gardens of Elysium
The Lightning Of Creation (2009)
Oil on canvas, 222x222mm

The Boundless Ocean
Adagio in a Key of Blue and Yellow (2017)
Oil on canvas, 222x222mm

And countless drawings of dubious relationship to the text in Quink Ink and a
Leonardt No. 41 nib.

Other written works by Mark Sheeky

as Author

365 Universes, Pentangel Books (2012)
The Many Beautiful Worlds of Death, Pentangel Books (2015)
Deep Dark Light (2018)

as Illustrator

Songs Of Life, Pentangel Books (2014)
Testing the Delicates, Ink Pantry Publishing (2017)

as Contributor

Hide It!, Mardibooks (2014)
The Ball of the Future, Earlyworks Press (2015)
Journeys Beyond, Earlyworks Press (2015)
Diversifly, Fair Acre Press (2018)

www.marksheeky.com

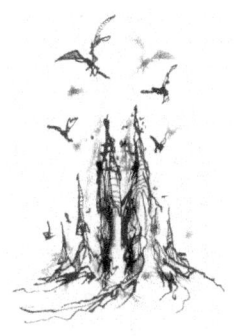